Praise for Tony Aspler and his previous books....

☆ ☆ ☆ ☆ ☆

Travels With My Corkscrew is an entertaining, anecdotal account of [Tony Aspler's] "drinking life" from the early 1960s to the present...
QUILL & QUIRE

Vintage Canada tells the history of Canadian wine, including insights into prohibition, it profiles all the existing wineries and includes copious tasting notes. This is essential reading for any Canadian who loves wine. We owe it to ourselves to discover our own viticultural heritage. We do have one.
WINETIDINGS MAGAZINE

Read [*Vintage Canada*] for entertainment, and keep it as an invaluable reference guide, because Aspler has tasted virtually every wine made in Canada and has rated each wine by vintage year.
THE OTTAWA CITIZEN

Tony Aspler, who is one of the most respected and knowledgeable wine educators around...has authored *Aligoté to Zinfandel*... It's all done in Aspler's easy, flowing, crystal-clear style, geared to answering consumers' simplest questions in straightforward, concise terms.
THE HAMILTON SPECTATOR

[Tony Aspler's] *Guide to New World Wines* points you to the better producers, and the front section has useful tips on food matching, cellaring and service. It's good to see Canadian wineries getting their share of coverage in this kind of internationally focused book.
THE GLOBE AND MAIL

Tony Aspler, Canada's best known wine writer, has a good introductory book called the *Wine Lover's Companion*. Written in a straightforward manner, the book covers everything from how wine is made to how it should be cellared and served.
THE FINANCIAL POST

Tony Aspler's *Aligoté to Zinfandel* is one of the best straight-forward, basic guides to wine I've ever seen...Practical, common sense, loads of information and a light reassuring touch make this a very useful book.
TODAY'S SENIORS

Memoirs of a wine lover

TONY ASPLER

FOREWORD BY HUGH JOHNSON

Travels with my Corkscrew

Memoirs of a wine lover

TONY ASPLER

FOREWORD BY HUGH JOHNSON

Travels with my Corkscrew

McGraw-Hill
Ryerson

Toronto Montréal New York Auckland Bogotá Caracas
Lisbon London Madrid Mexico Milan New Delhi San Juan
Singapore Sydney Tokyo

McGraw-Hill
Ryerson

300 Water Street, Whitby, Ontario L1N 9B6
http://www.mcgrawhill.ca

TRAVELS WITH MY CORKSCREW: Memoirs of a Wine Lover

ISBN: 0-07-560011-0

1 2 3 4 5 6 7 8 9 0 BBM 6 5 4 3 2 1 0 9 8 7

Printed and bound in Canada

Care has been taken to trace ownership of copyright material contained in this text;
however, the publisher will welcome any information that enables them to rectify any
reference or credit for subsequent editions.

Canadian Cataloguing in Publication Data

Aspler, Tony, 1939-

      Travels with my corkscrew: memoirs of a wine lover

ISBN 0-07-560011-0

1. Aspler, Tony, 1939-   2. Wine and wine making.

3. Authors, Canadian (English) - 20th century - Biography.*

I. Title.

TP547.A86A3 1997   641.2'2'092   C97-930986-7

PUBLISHER: Joan Homewood
EDITOR: Erin Moore
PRODUCTION COORDINATOR: Jennifer Burnell
EDITORIAL SERVICES: Barbara Brougham
COVER DESIGN & ILLUSTRATION: Sharon Matthews
INTERIOR DESIGN/COMPOSITION: Matthews Communications Design
PRINTER: Best Book Manufacturers
TYPEFACES: Berkeley Caflisch Script Regular

For
Marc and John Nadeau

Contents

Foreword

WITH EVERY ASPECT OF WINE SCRUTINIZED, EVERY BOTTLE ASSIGNED A status and every drop discussed, there remains one last angle on the subject still wrapped in an enigma; who are the hacks who set out to turn their predilection to profit; their thirst into a pension?

Tony Aspler is one of the frankest and funniest, the man from *The Toronto Star*, (via the BBC, CBC and assignments of all flavours) who has already painted vivid pictures of the wine-world in action in his detective novels, *The Beast of Barbaresco*, *Blood is Thicker than Beaujolais* and *Death on the Douro*.

Everyone learns about wine in his or her own way. Tony's way has been, shall we say, extremely human; richly mixed with real life, literary life, incident and accident in some unexpected parts of the world.

One of my favourite outrageous books about eating and drinking is A. J. Liebling's *Between Meals* — the joke being that for this incorrigible tucker-in there was effectively no such thing.

Aspler, I feel, is more self-controlled than this. In the back of his mind, if not the front, I suspect there is always the deadline (the only thing, that is, that gives us hacks our sense of direction — or indeed reality). He also has the itch to explain, the knack of imparting knowledge painlessly almost while looking the other way.

I take issue with him on some things. He chides the English with inventing the swizzle-stick (rightly or wrongly: it could just as well have been the French, or indeed the Russians). Yet he remains under the delusion that sparkling champagne was a French invention while on the contrary it was a happy discovery by the English.

But this is just the kind of thing that would provoke Tony into (well-lubricated) research — lead, I wouldn't be surprised, to another benign, rombustious volume.

I certainly hope so.

Hugh Johnson
SEPTEMBER 1997

Introduction

PICTURE IN YOUR MIND THE OLD JOKE OF THE FAT MAN SLIPPING ON A banana skin. Now substitute a bunch of grapes for the banana and you'll understand how wine was invented by accident.

Our primordial benefactor who first trod on grapes must have been something of a mystic. Whoever it was had no idea what he had spawned. *One small step for man, one giant libation for mankind.*

Imagine if that happy accident had never occurred. Or if the secret knowledge of fermentation had somehow become lost forever and we lived in a world without wine. How dull most dinner parties would be. How uninteresting most foods. No communion wine to celebrate Mass; no Manischewitz at the Passover table. No wine writers and no wine odysseys such as this one.

I use the term "wine writer" advisedly. I don't consider myself a wine critic, although I sometimes do have some harsh words to say about particular wines. Usually the space accorded to wine writing in newspapers and magazines is limited, and rather than tell readers what is bad I prefer to point them in the direction of the good stuff. In that sense I am a wine evangelist, since I believe that wine is a unique beverage that has afforded more pleasure and enlightenment down the ages than any other substance mankind has ever ingested. Let me put it this way: whom would you rather have to dinner — Napoleon Bonaparte who loved Chambertin or Adolf Hitler who was a teetotaler? Beethoven whose deathbed wish was for the wines of the Rhine or Tchaikovsky who only drank water and thought his head was falling off?

A friend of mine who imports wine into Ontario, Steven Trenholme, says he never drinks anything older than he is. "The body," he contends, "is a solera system. If you put something older into it, you'll get old. If you put something younger in it, you'll feel younger."

Maybe I have consumed too many old wines; arguably, the urge to write an autobiography is the first sign of senility. Since I still have all my organoleptic faculties about me, I have no desire to write my personal history. While this book contains many anecdotes about episodes in my life, its purpose is to share with you the pleasure I have derived from wine in a third of a century of chasing the grape around the world.

For the chapter headings of this book I have taken some liberties with quotations from notable wine lovers of the past. At least I imagine they were partial to the fermented grape. The people are real; their names have not been changed — to protect my innocence.

Travels with my Corkscrew

When the Bud Breaks

> "If Dionysus did not exist we would have to invent him"
>
> FRIEDRICH NIETZSCHE

First, let me explain how the Pope bought me a pair of shoes in Rome.

The year was 1985 and Pope John Paul was visiting Ontario. One Saturday morning in early summer I was having a meeting at my house in North Toronto with a wine importing agent, Ken Chase, regarding The Masters Games, a kind of Olympic Games for geri-athletes. We were discussing the possibility of setting up a wine fair as part of the cultural events that would be happening in the city as an adjunct to the sporting competitions.

The phone rang and Egon Foidl, the then Food & Beverage Director of the Sutton Place Hotel, asked to speak to Ken. He needed wine for the papal dinner that night. There was a note of urgency in his voice as if his future preferment within the company rested on his ability to secure desirable potables for the Pope.

John Paul was staying at Cardinal Carter's residence and the meals for the papal party were catered by the Sutton Place who also supplied the wines.

On the previous night the 11-member dinner party had demol-
ished a case of champagne and for that evening's meal Foidl needed six bottles of fine claret. To be specific, he was looking for six
bottles of an extraordinary wine, Château Mouton-Rothschild
1970.

"I don't have any Mouton '70," said Ken.
"Hold on, I'll ask Aspler if he's got some."

"I don't have Mouton," I replied, "but
I've got some Rausan-Ségla 1970 in my
cellar."

Nothing should distract the nose from analyzing a bouquet...

Now 1970 was one of the best years
for red Bordeaux since 1961, rivalled
since only by the 1982 vintage and possibly 1990 and 1996. I had bought several cases of 1970s when I returned to
Canada from England in 1976.

In 1970 Mouton-Rothschild was still a second growth (it was
elevated to first growth status with the 1973 vintage after years of
lobbying Comité Interprofessionel des Vins de Bordeaux by its
creator, Baron Guy de Rothschild). Château Rausan-Ségla, situated in the Margaux commune, was also a second growth but definitely not in the same class as the Mouton, in spite of the mag-
nificence of the vintage as a whole.

"Have you got six bottles?" asked Ken.

"Yes."

"Egon, would you accept Rausan-Ségla '70?"

Foidl, desperate for anything with 1970 on the label, agreed.

"How much do you want for them?" Ken asked me.

"I don't know. How much are they worth?" I replied.

"How about $85?"

"For the Pope, sure," I said.

Eighty-five dollars a bottle seemed very profitable considering
what I had paid for the wines in London eight years before. I reck-
oned the Vatican could afford $510 — but then I never found out

how much the hotel charged for my six bottles of Rausan-Ségla. (In 1984, to give you an idea of the Liquor Control Board of Ontario's general list prices for claret, Château d'Angludet 1979 was selling for $17.85, Château Kirwan 1979 for $21.20, and Château Montlabert 1981 for $13.20.)

A week later I was flying to Rome to receive an award for wine writing — Premio Internazionale di Giornalismo, Il fiore dei vini, sponsored by Casa Vinicola Umberto Fiore. The prize was a silver plaque and, curiously, a wooden cigarette box with an engraved silver top, depicting a cobbled village street in Gattinara.

I felt that it was only fitting for me to spend the money I had received for the papal wine in the Eternal City. I needed a new pair of shoes, so I went into a shoe store and bought myself an expensive pair of black loafers. The leather was like butter.

I only hope that Pope John Paul enjoyed drinking my wine as much as I enjoyed wearing his shoes.

*C*igarettes *are frowned on at wine tastings. Nothing should distract the nose from analyzing a bouquet, be it a woman's perfume, a man's after-shave, flowers on the table, the smell of smoke or, worse, butt-filled ash-trays. Most wine professionals don't wear fragrance of any kind and the sensitivity of their noses detects it on the casual passer-by.*

Yet when you travel in France and Italy, invariably you come across winemakers who smoke like fire trucks. In fact, I have tasted wines from the barrel in Burgundy with a vintner who held a cigarette in the nicotine-stained fingers of one hand while he sipped from a tasting glass in the other.

Smokers tell me that their habit does not impair their ability to taste and evaluate wine. They contend that they are used to tasting through the overlay of tar and nicotine, that their palates have adjusted and somehow compensated for the flavour of tobacco.

And as smokers tend to justify their habit and downplay its effect on their tasting abilities, non-smokers can get self-righteous about seeking a sterile environment. Perhaps we should go the whole hog and have showers installed in tasting rooms.

I recall once when Jim White was writing restaurant reviews for the Toronto Star *we were both (independently) in a new spot on Wellington Street, called Avanti. Jim could not abide the smell of perfume while he was eating. In fact, as a food critic he believed there should not only be smoke-free zones in restaurants, but perfume-free zones as well. At the table behind him was a woman who had fairly bathed in the latest designer scent: its fragrance billowed from her like crashing waves. Halfway through his first course Jim rose and went over to the table. He asked her if she would move because her perfume was preventing him from tasting his food.*

The woman was so stunned, she did.

I come by it honestly, my love of wine, even though I didn't recognize my all-consuming passion until I was in my mid-twenties. I must have been in denial through my teen years, but the seeds of the grape were there in childhood.

...the seeds of the grape were there in childhood.

My sister reminded me recently how my mother used to cajole me into going to the dentist. I have always had a horror of dentists, even though they are, as a profession, the most gentle of people and probably the most dedicated class of oenophiles. More dentists have invested in wineries or laid down magnificent cellars than any other group, including doctors.

My dentist phobia is one of two memorable results of my being fostered out to a family in Hudson, Quebec, during the war years when my mother, on her own and working in Montreal, could not look after my sister and me. My foster mother used to say, "If you're naughty I'll send you to the dentist." Naturally, whenever my own mother suggested it was time for me to go for a check-up, I would dissolve into paroxysms of tears. At the age of five, my sister reminded me, I would hang onto the table leg in the kitchen and scream as she and my mother tried to reason with me. And then Mum would resort to bribery.

The only thing that would prise my hands from the table leg was the promise of grapes. If she gave me a bunch of grapes I would accompany her to the dentist, albeit grudgingly, munching tearfully along the way. Years later a dentist explained to me that eating the amount of grapes I did accounted for the many fillings I have in my mouth.

I should have waited until their natural sugar had been fermented into alcohol.

My chief other memory of that time in Hudson is being taught French by the nuns. The only two phrases I came back to Montreal with were, "J'ai fini" and "Mange le merde." My mother, who spoke no French, was extremely proud of her bilingual son and had me lisp out the two phrases I had learned to her lady friends at tea.

My mother's lack of French had consequences later in life. She relied on the linguistic abilities of my stepfather, a lawyer who spoke French and German and taught himself Italian to attend a wedding in Sicily (more of that later). As a student at McGill I was living at home and one day the phone rang and my mother answered it. I could hear her replying enthusiastically, "Oui...oui...oui...oui..." Knowing she could not understand what she was listening to, I came into the living room. She put her hand over the receiver and whispered to me, "I think it's a friend of your father's having a joke...oui...oui."

After a few more minutes of this my mother began to frown and handed me the phone. I listened to the voice on the other end and then put the receiver down.

The caller, encouraged by my mother's frequent affirmatives, was indulging in a string of obscene fantasies.

As every wine lover knows, wine is an endless journey, charged with as much anguish, exhilaration, disappointment and rapture as life itself. For me the quest began when I was bitten by a grape. It was in the spring of 1964. I was living in London, England, in a one-bedroom apartment off Marylebone High Street. The former tenant had painted the walls of the corridor purple, the kitchen blood-red and the separate toilet orange. This tiny space, with its plastic chandelier and musical toilet roll, looked like a throne room. The bathroom and the bedroom were all mirrored and, judging from the phone calls I received for the first three months after I moved in, the chromatically-challenged occupant before me made a tidy living in the missionary position.

I was working for BBC Radio at the time, writing the script for a daily rolling home show called "Roundabout." For a short time I shared a small office with John Cleese at the BBC's radio variety studios, Aeolian Hall on Bond Street. John, in his pre–silly walk era, had just come down from Cambridge. He was one of several writer/performers from the university's Footlights revue who had been hired by "Aunty" to write a series called, "I'm Sorry I'll Read That Again." This radio show turned out to be the prototype for the future BBC-TV series, "Monty Python's Flying Circus."

...wine is an endless journey...

Living alone in London, I learned to cook. Then one day in March 1964, I decided I needed a hobby. Wine seemed the natural adjunct to cooking, an enterprise I took very seriously in my blood-red kitchen — though more as an aid to seduction than a gastronomic end in itself.

The question was, how do you get into wine? I had a friend named Lionel Frumkin, a fourth-generation English wine merchant, who was writing a book entitled *The Science and Technique of Wine*. He was working for a wine importing company in London named Southard's and had spent three years on the

Continent, researching with Delor in Bordeaux, Bouchard Père et Fils in Beaune, Hugel in Riquewihr, Deinhard in Koblenz and Lagenbach in Worms.

Lionel used to take me to the wine auctions at Christie's where together we would buy incredible Burgundies at knock-down prices. I still remember paying 17/6d (some $3) a bottle for 1964 Grivelet Vosne Romanée and 25 shillings a bottle for that shipper's Grands Échézeaux. (In the late 1960s an American friend, Ray Smart, whom I introduced to the Christie's wine auctions, bought six bottles of 1865 Lafite, which auctioneer Michael Broadbent referred to as a five-star year, "the second half of the first great pre-phylloxera twin vintages." Ray sold me one of the precious bottles at the prorated price he had paid for the lot. It cost me £18. I could buy a car with what that bottle would cost today! Incidentally, as I describe in the next chapter, I did drink it).

Lionel Frumkin suggested that the best way to learn about wine was to lay down a cellar. I had no idea what this meant — let alone how to go about it. Enterprising wine merchant that he was, Lionel was prepared to make the selection of bottles for me. All I had to do was come up with the cash. By this time I was sharing an apartment in Maida Vale with my oldest friend, Bernard Silver, who ran an advertising company with his brother from a building on Gray's Inn Road. In the basement was an abandoned wine cellar complete with rusting metal racks. I talked Bernie into putting money into the venture too, but we were still shy of the amount Lionel suggested we needed to have an interesting, wide-ranging selection of red Bordeaux, which were enticingly inexpensive in those days.

Among other expatriate Canadians living in England during the 1960s was a beautiful young woman from Hamilton, Cindy Bury, who was the Bunny Mother at the London Playboy Club. She was living with a dentist named John Riley whose show-business practice included the Beatles and Roman Polanski (John made the fangs for Polanski's movie, *Dracula*). John Riley, who liked the good life, was eager to participate in the cellar scheme, so we all stumped up £200 each. I can't recall how many cases we purchased for our money, but the wall of claret sure looked impressive in the racks of Bernie's office cellar. Lionel had given each of us a list of the wines, suggesting how long we should keep the bottles before opening them to avoid disappointment. I don't think even he realized how long the 1961 vintage would last.

Suffice it to say, my third of the cellar was consumed long before it should have been. Bernie was less impulsive about pulling corks, while John Riley seemed to have forgotten that he owned four bottles from each case that were lying in the cellar under Gray's Inn Road, gradually losing their labels because the area was far too damp. When Bernie and I reminded him, he said he was happy to let the wine age and increase in value.

Well, Dionysus is a perverse god.

...Dionysus is a perverse god

Bernie and I eyed John's portion of claret with envy as we saw the prices of his wines rising as our minuscule stock diminished. In 1973, a year before the wine bubble burst and prices plummeted, Bernie moved his business out of the Gray's Inn Road building and told John repeatedly to come and collect his wines. John did not come and the removal men must have done the job for him because when he finally did turn up the building and the cellar were completely empty. And the removal company swore up and down that they knew nothing about bottles of wine in the basement.

Apart from investing in a cellar and buying wine at auction, I was also devouring wine books by the yard and making visits to the vineyards of France, Spain and Portugal to learn more about the subject. By the mid-1960s, with Carnaby Street and the King's Road in full swing, I was working as a reporter for the BBC

Radio's national morning show, "Today." Knowing of my interest in wine, the assignment editor would send me to cover any story that was remotely connected with beverage alcohol. My greatest moment came when I was invited to the 90th birthday lunch for the legendary gastronome, André Simon, the founder of the International Wine & Food Society. The event was held at The White House Restaurant, within walking distance of Broadcasting House in London. I was told to get an interview with the great man.

There is an apocryphal story about André Simon, author of more seminal books on wine and food than anyone has the right to have written. At the conclusion of a class on wine appreciation, his students decided to play a joke on him. They took a decanter and poured in equal amounts of 1928 and 1929 Château Mouton-Rothschild. They handed him the wine and asked him to identify it blind. The grand old man poured himself a glass, inspected the colour, swirled the wine and sniffed the bouquet. Then he took some, swished it around his mouth and thought for a second. Pointing to his left cheek, he said, "Mouton '28." Then he pointed to his right cheek. "Mouton '29."

I wish I still had the menu from that lunch. I recall it started with champagne because that was André Simon's favourite drink (he wrote an eloquent history on the subject in 1962). And then into fine Burgundies... Carried away by the spirit of the occasion, I guess, I imbibed more champagne and Burgundy than I was accustomed to, especially on an empty stomach. I don't recall what we had to eat at that celebratory lunch, nor did I have the presence of mind to turn on the tape recorder when André Simon got up to reply to the birthday toast. At least, I think that's what happened. I took a taxi back to Broadcasting House. When the producer of the day (a renowned xenophobe who masqueraded as a Little Englander) asked for the tape, I mumbled that the old boy spoke in French which would have been incomprehensible to ninety-five per cent of our audience.

To further my wine knowledge I joined The Sunday Times Wine Club, which was run by Hugh Johnson, and the first wine I purchased was Masi Valpolicella. I went to as many tastings as I could weasel my way into (I was not part of the wine trade whose members were distinguished by their ability to hit a spittoon with a laser-like jet of wine from five paces, nor was I an accredited wine journalist). With the arrogance of youth I thought I understood wine, once I had got over the embarrassment of ordering a half bottle of Rheingau Auslese with a grilled trout at a restaurant on Charlotte Street. The waiter, who probably knew less about wine than I did, didn't bat an eyelash as I consumed this unhappy marriage with the stoicism of one who is not willing to acknowledge in public that he has made a ghastly mistake. I would have liked to tell you that I had accidentally discovered a unique wine and food pairing, as delicious as Münster cheese and Alsace Gewürztraminer or Sauternes and foie gras, but I had not.

A little knowledge, they say, is a dangerous thing, especially when you are prepared to put it on the line in a blind tasting. By the early 1970s I had consumed more wine than the national average and considered myself, if not an expert, at least a connoisseur. I could read through a wine list and pronounce the names correctly. (In those days English wine lists consisted mainly of claret, hock (i.e. anything from Germany), Burgundy white and red, Chianti, and Mateus Rosé. The New World, let alone Languedoc-Roussillon, did not exist oenologically.) I could tell the difference between a red Bordeaux and a red Burgundy by the shape of the bottle if not the bouquet (or "nose"). I had read the literature, kept up to date with early issues of *Decanter* magazine. I was ready, I believed, to enter a wine tasting competition.

I was ready to enter a wine tasting competition.

The event was organized by a wine club, one of several of which I was now a card-carrying member. In order to qualify for the blind tasting part you had answer twenty multiple-choice questions and send in your answers. This was a breeze since I had acquired an extensive library of wine books and nowhere in the rules did it say that the written test was not an open book affair.

The tasting was held in the cellars of a wine merchant, by candlelight for some reason. A dozen or so competitors were given a series of glasses of wine served blind and had to answer questions about them. The first wine was a petit château Bordeaux (I learned later) and we were asked to identify the region it came from. I didn't have a clue. I put down "Beaujolais."

I was seated next to a man who was several years younger than I. He was holding the wine up to the candle, studying its colour against the background of a sheet of white paper. He sniffed and he swirled, sniffed again and swirled. Then he took a sip and gnawed on the wine as a dog might chew on a bone. And then he spat on the concrete floor. Charming, I thought. He turned out to be a member of the Oxford University wine tasting society and went on to win the competition.

I obviously needed to study more. Then, quite fortuitously, I met the man who was to become my mentor in the wine business. His name was Gordon Bucklitsch and I ran into him on my first visit to Champagne in 1974. Gordon was a latter-day Falstaff, a huge man with a head of flowing white hair, a booming voice and an infinite capacity for enjoying life.

Gordon had no use for corks. Once a wine or a bottle of sherry or port was opened, he threw away the cork. When I met him in the cellars of Pommery & Greno (as the champagne house was then called) he was the director of the Grant's of St. James's Wine School. On our return to London he suggested that I might like to monitor the course he and other lecturers gave for new members of the wine trade.

As a freelance broadcaster working for BBC, CBC and

Australian radio I had the luxury of choosing my own hours. I blocked off three days for the course and sat through full days of lectures on all aspects of wine and winemaking.

Gordon introduced the subject with his historical perspective: his thesis was that wine was the major influence on the course of English history. Now you may think that this is carrying one's pre-occupation to the loony end of logic; but a case can be made to support his argument.

Key international agreements and alliances by royal marriage were contracted, he argued, to maintain the uninterrupted flow of wine into Britain. In 1152, the nineteen-year-old Henry Plantagenet married the thirty-year-old Eleanor of Aquitaine and two years later they ruled England as King Henry II and Queen Eleanor. This dynastic merger brought the vineyards of Bordeaux under English control for three hundred years, a happy circum-stance that created the Englishman's love of claret. The Methuen Treaty with the Portuguese in 1703 set a stiff tariff on French wines and gave preferential treatment to Portuguese wines at a time when the modern style of port was emerging. The Englishman's passion for vintage port results from that trading advantage under the treaty.

Gordon Bucklitsch had served in the British Navy during World War II and much of his wine lore and language evolved from that experience. I remember him describing the nose of a Margaux as smelling of "tarred rope." I could only smell wine, and wondered how he could characterize the nose in such terms.

Having conducted hundreds of wine tastings I know that this is the most daunting aspect of wine appreciation for the neophyte — how to find the words to describe a smell. And even before that, how to break down a bouquet into its component parts of oak, fruit character and the organic smells that happen when wine is aged. (You really can detect such smells as truffles, leather, coffee beans, bitter chocolate, seaweed and iodine in older reds. It just takes practice. The nose is like a muscle; the more you use it the more developed and acute it becomes. Women are better at this smelling business than men, being more accustomed to using their noses to select fragrances for their bodies and spices for their casseroles. Another difference is that women can maintain their nasal acuity until well into the evening, whereas we reach our peak by noon after which it's all down hill.

Women are better at this smelling business than men...

Which is probably why most professional tastings are held in the mornings.)

Gordon Bucklitsch was a master at distinguishing the bouquets of the different Bordeaux communes. To his students they all smelled the same, but by the end of the course we could tell Pauillac (blackcurrant and cigar box) from Pomerol (cedar and blueberry). He also taught me an invaluable lesson in self-preservation. After our visit to Champagne we drove to Calais to take the ferry across the English Channel to Dover. This narrow stretch of water can suddenly and without warning become a mariner's nightmare. A Force 9 gale blew up and the passengers hung over the railings of the ferry, losing their lunch. Gordon instructed me to follow him below deck to the bar. I was feeling somewhat queasy, and all the more so when he ordered a bottle of champagne and two glasses.

"Drink," he said, handing me a glass. "You'll feel better."

We stayed in the bar drinking champagne for the entire crossing and I was right as rain.

I have much to thank him for; not the least of which is my fictional wine writer-detective, Ezra Brant, the on-going hero of three murder mysteries so far. Ezra, with his magpie mind and jovial presence, is modelled on the late Gordon Bucklitsch.

*I*n the wine world there are certain truths that cannot be challenged. They are Holy Writ as if they came down with Moses and the tablets from the mountain.

The first is: wine always tastes better in the presence of the winemaker. Maybe it's our natural civility or a sense of good manners. But it's true. Taste the same wine on your own and your judgement of it will be less ecstatic.

Just as you don't say to a beaming mother that her newborn babe looks like Benito Mussolini, you don't spit the wine at the feet of the winemaker and declare it fit only for washing the car. Maybe you'd like to, but you don't.

The second basic truth about wine is: the bottle you drop in your cellar is always your best bottle. Anyone who has ever laid down a cellar will tell you that until you have dropped a bottle and watched it smash on the floor the enterprise has not been properly inaugurated. Call it the Bacchic Imperative, but there must be at least one bottle that becomes a libation for the gods.

When I built (or more correctly had The Wine Establishment build) my dream cellar in the basement of my old house in North Toronto, with its cathedral-worthy Gothic door (to the cellar, that is, not the house), I moved the bottles carefully into the racks. I put the best wines that needed longest cellaring at the bottom. Then those for short-term ageing and current consumption above them.

I had almost finished when one of the bottles, a simple California red, slipped through my fingers and fell to the tiled floor.

Ironically it remained intact. But it bounced and struck the neck of a 1976 Pernand-Vergelesses shipped by Joseph Drouhin. The Burgundy bottle cracked open and the cellar floor was christened.

Champagne

> "Champagne makes people lose their heads."
> MADAME DEFARGE

The French say that champagne is the wine a young man drinks on the evening of his first mistake. Perhaps he should drink it on the morning after, by way of atonement, champagne being the only alcoholic beverage you can consume at breakfast without people looking sideways at you. Certainly, for celebration or remorse there is no better wine.

I courted my first wife with champagne and kippers. (Bizarre, yes, but if the champagne is dry enough it does work — even if the marriage ultimately did not. Incidentally, I proposed to her in 1969 over a bottle of Château Haut Brion 1958, a vintage Michael Broadbent characterized as "curiously attractive but frequently maligned." I often wonder if the quality of the year I chose sowed the seeds of marital destruction from the start.)

If my doctor were to tell me that I had to give up all wines but one for the rest of my life, the one I would choose without hesitation would be champagne. After all, what other wine can you drink at any hour of the day or night, and what other wine is so versatile when it comes to matching with food? The range of styles is spectacular, from the lemony-tart Blanc de Blancs of Salon and the undosed sparklers of Laurent-Perrier to the toasty, mouth-filling richness of a vintage Krug; from Billecart-Salmon rosé, whose colour, coincidentally enough, truly is salmon and which tastes of wild strawberries, to the Demi-sec of Pol Roger that goes so well with Christmas pudding. Then you have the opportunity of trying the less gaseous Crémant of Besserat de Bellefon that goes so well with quenelles de brochet and fresh coulommiers or a still Coteaux champenois. And if you develop a yen for red wine, there is always the still Bouzy Rouge of Bollinger that you can serve with carbonnades de boeuf flammande.

...the best time to drink champagne? Before, during and after.

Alain de Vogüé, the chairman of Veuve Clicquot-Ponsardin until 1987, best summed up the wine's versatility in his succinct answer to my question, when is the best time to drink champagne? His reply: "Before, during and after."

For the Comtesse de Maigret, the best time was 11 o'clock in the morning, with thinly cut cucumber sandwiches. She told me this in 1976 as we sat in Moët & Chandon's Orangerie sipping the remains of a bottle of 1911 that had been disgorged that morning to impress some visiting English wine merchants. The wine had lost its bubbles but it still had its wonderfully yeasty flavour and tasted remarkably fresh, rather like a well aged white Chassagne-Montrachet.

She told me the story of how her late husband single-handedly saved France from a diplomatic embarrassment with the Russians. In 1960 Krushchev and his entourage visited France. While her husband was busy with meetings, Mrs. K. was taken for a tour of a movie studio where the film *"Can-Can"* with Shirley MacLaine was being shot. The good lady was so offended at the sight of chorus girls kicking up their legs and showing their bloomers that she had to be escorted out. To repair the damage a tour of Möet & Chandon's cellars was hastily arranged, and the Comte de Maigret suddenly found himself host to one hundred Russians.

In honour of Krushchev's visit, he ordered the cellar master to disgorge sufficient bottles of the Russian leader's birth year (1894) to serve to the party. The Comte watched sadly as the Russians guzzled down the rare old champagne like vodka.

That evening the Comtesse de Maigret entertained me and a group of English wine merchants to dinner. It was the year of the American Bicentennial and Moët had prepared a special cuvée to celebrate the event. Two ceremonial bottles, dressed with crossed stars and stripes on the neck, were presented to all of us in a plastic carrying case that looked as if it held a trumpet.

I had to return to London the next day — a London that was in the midst of a terrorist bombing campaign by the IRA. Their favourite targets were railway stations, which caused maximum injury, disruption and fear.

I had to fly from Paris to Gatwick Airport and take the train to London. In one hand I was carrying a suitcase and shoulder bag; in the other, the case of champagne. The London train was at the platform when I arrived at Gatwick and was just about to leave. I had to run to catch it. My shoulder bag must have brushed against the clip fastener of the case which held the champagne. The lid flew open and the two bottles of Möet fell to the platform and exploded.

I have never seen a railway station empty so fast.

I was left standing on the deserted platform, staring down at the wreckage of broken glass and the spreading puddle of sparkling wine.

I could have wept.

It was Robert Fulford, as editor of *Saturday Night* magazine, who gave me my first break as a wine writer. In 1975 he commissioned me to write a piece about wine. I was working as a CBC radio producer in London at the time (from my office window I could see Lionel Frumkin's father's wine shop on Great Titchfield Street). Since I was not supposed to be doing freelance writing outside the Corporation, I wrote the piece under a pseudonym.

I had thought of calling myself Bermuda Schwartz but this seemed to be too frivolous for the subject matter. Instead I chose the name Perry Anders. This was meant to be a joke, but the reference was so arcane that only devotees of the London Times crossword puzzle might have caught it. (Periander ruled Corinth for 40 years from 625 BC and his only claim to fame was that he introduced into that city a festival of Dionysus.)

I came across my carbon copy of that original article, the first page of which I'd like to share with you to show how a callow young wine writer got around the problem of having to write about wine.

... all is not necessarily what it says on the label...

When I was in Cairo in 1965, en route for the ancient Ptolemaic vineyards of Gianaclis west of the Nile Delta (incidentally, the largest single vineyard in the world after California), I was stopped by a local mafioso who offered to show me, among other oriental delights, a sight jealously guarded from all but the most discriminating tourist. It turned out to be two human skulls, one smaller than the other and both looking as if they had seen better days. "This," said my guide, in a voice trembling with pecuniary anticipation, "is the skull of Cleopatra...and this one is the skull of Cleopatra as a young girl."

That experience has stood me in good stead when it comes to judging wines, because in this less than perfect world all is not necessarily what it says on the label, as recent history will attest. Remember the claret scandal in Bordeaux last year (passing off vin ordinaire as

noble Médoc, St. Émilion and Graves)? And the fuss at Oporto (for-
tifying the fermenting grape juice with coal-based alcohol rather
than brandy)? Not that the French and Portuguese are the only wine-
growers who, for quick profits, have "salted the soup"...

As a staff member of CBC living in London it was incumbent
upon me to come back to Canada after four years, rather like
a diplomatic posting. I was assigned by the Head of Current
Affairs in Toronto to create a national music programme for the
Stereo Network. (Until that time the morning slot was filled by
local announcers across the country who acted as classical disc
jockeys.) The fact that a three-hour morning music programme
came under the Current Affairs department rather than Radio
Music speaks volumes about the political in-fighting at the
Corporation in those days. (It's probably no different now.)

I flew to Toronto in November 1976, the day that René
Lévesque's Parti québécois won the Quebec election, and moved
into the Chelsea Inn while I looked for a house to rent. That
weekend was Grey Cup weekend. Out-of-town fans, filled with
the spirit of the occasion, were passing footballs down the hall
outside my room at 3 a.m. I wondered what I had come back to.

That Saturday night I had been invited to dinner in Burlington
by a friend from McGill days who had lived for a time in London
while I was there. Stuart Smith had been a top debater at college
as well as a brilliant student; he had studied psychiatry but had
given it up for politics. He was then the leader of the opposition
Liberal Party. I can't recall who else was at that dinner but I
remember clearly being served my first Ontario wine on Canadian
soil. It was Inniskillin Vin Nouveau 1974, a Maréchal Foch, the
very first wine Karl Kaiser and Donald Ziraldo had produced.

"This is the best wine made in Canada," said Stuart.

I tasted it and said nothing. I was thinking of those fourteen
cases of 1970 Bordeaux I had purchased prior to leaving England

which would be shipped over along with my car, furniture and household effects.

I was singularly ill-equipped to be a music producer. I had no musical training whatsoever, apart from playing the trumpet in the Epsom College corps band at the age of sixteen. By joining the band you got out of having to carry (and clean) a rifle. Our debut as a brass ensemble was planned for the end-of-term festivities in the hall known as Big School. Following the headmaster's announcements we were to play "God Save the Queen" and the school would sing along. We were halfway through the anthem before the assembly recognized what we were playing.

The host of the CBC radio programme was Eric Friesen, a lover of music and baseball with a rich radio voice. The format I had devised infuriated many CBC listeners and there were constant letters in the papers decrying the fact that there was talk in the morning. The music was broken up by reviews, interviews and editorials about the arts. The final hour, after the 8 a.m. news until nine o'clock, was devoted to longer interviews and documentaries. On Friday I initiated "Breakfast with Friesen," during which a celebrity guest was invited to have breakfast on-air with Eric — a breakfast that consisted of bagels, lox and cream cheese, strawberries and champagne. The champagne we ordered was Möet & Chandon White Star because it was the cheapest at the time.

The concept was novel enough to attract guests of the calibre of Peter Ustinov and Maureen Forrester to these breakfasts. But the CBC brass was uneasy about champagne being consumed in studio, especially at 8 in the morning.

The only reason they allowed me to continue the practice was that it would cost us much more than the price of a bottle of champagne to pay the interview fee of the guests we wanted on the show.

The whole thing blew up, however, when Eric went on leave,

and I had to post a job application notice for a temporary host on the notice board in the announcers' office. At the end of the list of qualifications and abilities I was looking for in a programme host, I added "...and must be able to drink champagne at 8 a.m. on a Friday morning."

Now you would have thought that this would have raised a smile at least, but instead the head of the department had to deal with an outraged CUPE, the announcers' union, since one of their members had filed a grievance against the show for being "frivolous."

N ow *this* is frivolous. There is an ancient wager involving the consumption of champagne which I heard about in London many years ago. I don't know how or when the bet originated although I imagine it must have been in the early nineteenth century.

The bet is: you have to drink three bottles of champagne, run three miles and make love to three women in three hours.

Couched in these terms it was obviously devised by a man for other men, but in these days of equal opportunity it could also be open for women challengers. Who knows, it might even become an Olympic sport. If ballroom dancing can make it, anything is possible.

I have never attempted this exploit, although in some idle moments on plane trips I have thought about how one might go about the logistics in order to accomplish it. What do you do first? Run a mile, drink a bottle of champagne and then make love?

The sensualist would make love to the three women, drink the three bottles of champagne and then attempt to run the three miles.

The hedonist would drink a bottle of champagne, make love, drink another bottle, make love and repeat.

The athlete would run the three miles and leave the champagne till last.

The major stumbling block would be: who holds the stop-watch?

I first used this idea as a chapter in a novel that never got published. It was called *Body English* and was highly derivative of Mordecai Richler's *The Apprenticeship of Duddy Kravitz*. Then I tried to use it as the basis of a screenplay, a farce set on board a transatlantic liner. The young, feckless hero accepts the bet and goes into training. Soon other passengers get wind of the bet and there is furious activity as odds are laid and money changes hands. Just as he is about to embark upon his Herculean task a storm blows up...

Regarding the bet, I should give one of those television car commercial caveats: "Do not try this stunt at home."

Curiously, Möet & Chandon's White Star champagne has played more than a minor role in my life. My last major assignment as a CBC producer before I left the Corporation in 1981 was "Africa Week." This was the brain-child of Bernie Lucht, currently the Executive Producer of "Ideas." Since Bernie was busy with his commitments to the "Ideas" series, I was put in charge of what turned out to be a two-year project.

"Africa Week" was a mammoth undertaking — four hours of radio over five consecutive nights to give listeners an insight into the politics, economics, social and cultural life of contemporary Africa. Harry Rasky was the host and Anne Walmsley the researcher.

A team of four producers — Bernie, Steve Wadhams, George Somerwill and I — each spent several weeks in different parts of Africa, tape-recording material and gathering information.

My "night" dealt with French West Africa and I travelled around Senegal, the Ivory Coast, Cameroon and what used to be called Zaire for six weeks. The other producers were old Africa hands who had worked there with CIDA. I had never been south of Egypt and had no idea what to expect. Those six weeks turned out to be the most magical I have ever spent. The people, the colours, the sounds, the extraordinary vistas made a lasting impression on me.

Part of my work was to record authentic tribal music and when I was in Abidjan, the capital of the Ivory Coast, I contacted the Canadian High Commission to find out how best to go about this. Obviously, they had had such requests before because a commercial attaché told me how to do it.

"Put 25,000 CFA ($140) in an envelope and I'll drive you to the village," he told me. "By the way, if you want to skate, they have an Olympic size rink in the Hôtel d'Ivoire. The only people who use it are Canadians and Americans and one local guy who studied medicine at McGill. You can't miss him, he wears a Montreal Canadiens' hockey jersey."

Songon M'Brathe is the second oldest established village in the Ivory Coast after Cocody which is now an expensive suburb of the capital and the site of the Hôtel d'Ivoire. It's about an hour's drive from Abidjan, a turn off from the main coastal highway along a mud-packed road lined with tall palm trees. The villagers work as a co-operative, raising cocao, cola nuts and palm oil. By the time I arrived there, with Oliver Jalbert from the Canadian embassy, a man from the Ministry of Tourism and an interpreter, the village chief and elders had assembled in the dusty square in front of whitewashed buildings with their tin roofs and shuttered windows painted aquamarine. For this ceremonial welcome, the men were swathed in gorgeously coloured robes which they wore with great dignity over sports shirts you only see in Miami Beach. The elders, about twelve of them, carried five-foot-long gold-painted staffs surmounted by carvings of lions and elephants. On their heads they wore black pill-box hats encircled with gold emblems of moons, squares and triangles. Gold chains dangled from their necks to their navels and their fingers were heavy with gold rings like sunbursts and elaborately wrought bangles. Behind them stood a second line of men, shorter in stature, wearing less colourful robes, black homburgs and no jewellery.

The chief and two of his sons wore gold sunglasses but instead of coloured lenses they peered through a mesh of gold wire. The chief himself, who reminded me of Kirby Puckett, was dressed in the finest and most colourful robes of all and on his head he wore a gold and red velvet crown that looked eerily like the one on the label of St. Stephen's Crown Cabernet Sauvignon from Hungary. His staff, more elaborate than the others as befitted his station, was of carved ivory and ebony with a long golden end that looked like the horn of a unicorn. On its pommel was a carving of a roaring lion and a man with his hand upon its mane.

The chief did not speak but one of his advisers spoke for him, a kind of official greeter. After the ritual exchange of gifts (I gave him a CBC decal and he gave me a bag made from spliced palm fronds) I slipped him the envelope which disappeared under his robe. With a wave of his staff the music began and the entire village began to dance. A huge drum supported on a pole carried on the shoulders of two men provided the bass beat as the villagers shook seed-filled gourds, beat buffalo horns and blew into large wooden flutes. The square was alive with dancing feet as the dust rose and the music echoed off the wall of green behind.

..the music began and the entire village began to dance.

The only person who did not seem to be enjoying the occasion was the medicine man who had eyed me with suspicion ever since my arrival in the village. He was dressed in a heavy, all-encompassing cape that reached the ground, fashioned from long strands of corn-braided straw, and on his head was a straw bonnet tied under his chin that looked like a blond fright wig.

When the dancing had finished and I had recorded at least an hour of music, the chief invited me to have lunch with him. A table for six had been set under the palm trees at the edge of a lagoon. Silver cutlery and the best china gleamed on the gingham tablecloth. There were crown-capped litre bottles of red wine on the table, along with beer and soft drinks.

The entire village sat in the sun and watched us as we ate. The chief had removed his robe and his shirt and sat bare-chested, asking me in mellifluous French about my work at CBC.

A meat and fish stew in a hot sauce arrived and was served with *foutu*, bananas and plantain cooked with manioc and yams, a kind of couscous to accompany the main dish. The chief asked me if I had ever tasted palm wine. When I told him I had not, he ordered two glasses which arrived in no time at all. It came in a plastic petrol can. The liquid was a pearly, opalescent colour. It looked like sperm.

I took a tentative sniff. It smelled like rubber. I tasted it. It was slightly effervescent and tasted of palm oil. It was bitter, grassy and rubbery — more Goodyear than good year.

The expression on my face, though I tried to hide it, made the chief roar with laughter.

"We will drink something more to your taste," he said.

He clapped his hands and an aide approached. There was a whispered consultation and the man disappeared only to return a moment later with fresh glasses, and a bottle of Moët & Chandon White Star and Laurent-Perrier champagne arrived, suitably chilled.

The aide filled large tumblers to the brim and I watched the chief chug-a-lug the champagne with great relish, rivulets of it running down his barrel chest.

The second village we visited was Abo Bote with a population of about three thousand. It appeared more prosperous than Songon M'Brathe because of its two-storey houses. The chief's house was very spacious and had an air-conditioner set into the wall. Two televisions stood on a table in the corner, one on top of the other, next to a decorated plastic Christmas tree (although it was the fourth week of March). Again champagne was produced, but the chief's assistant had not yet mastered the technique of opening the bottle. He was trying to remove the cork without first having untwisted the wire muzzle. When he finally wrestled the cork free, it shot out of the bottle like a howitzer, sending a fountain of wine all over Madame Brisebois, a woman deputy who was our guide for the tour of her village. The poor woman was soaked from head to toe and to add insult to injury there was only enough champagne for the chief, Oliver Jalbert and myself to have a glass.

There I was, in the middle of the African bush, drinking chilled champagne for the second time in one day. And then it occurred to me. This was the true French colonial legacy: love of champagne.

O f all alcoholic beverages champagne is the most abused. Not only has the New World co-opted the name and used it for anything that sparkles (except for Oregon and New Zealand, bless them), but victorious sports teams use it as shampoo.

The British long ago took their revenge on the French for having invented the best drink in the world. They came up with the swizzle stick. Small enough to dangle from a watch chain, this infernal machine, which looks like the skeletal frame of a Lilliputian umbrella, is used expressly to remove the bubbles that the champenois laboured so long to put into the wine. If you want a champagne without fizz, either buy Coteaux champenois, the still wine of the region, so acid that it could take the enamel off your teeth, or opt for a white wine from the Jura or the Savoie instead.

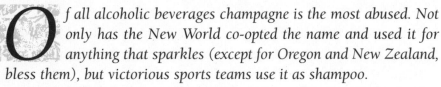

Of all alcoholic beverages champagne is the most abused.

Even more perfidious than the swizzle stick is another English invention: the champagne coupe, that shallow bird bath of a glass that has become the symbol of champagne itself. The only worse receptacle for a sparkling wine is a Wellington boot. In such a glass the shallow lake of wine warms up quickly and goes flat in no time at all. You don't see the upward passage of the bubbles, and each time you take a sip the circumference of the glass is so large you get far too much sparkling wine and it foams in the mouth.

I read somewhere that the coupe glass was designed for Queen Victoria who found that the bubbles in champagne induced flatulence. The object of the saucer-shaped glass, aided by the swizzle stick, was to help the wine lose its gas in short order.

(Queen Victoria also managed to ruin two more of the world's finest beverages by adding Lochnagar malt whisky to claret.)

The ideal glass for champagne is an elegant, tall flute of clear, thin glass whose diameter at the aperture is no more than an inch and a half. This means that you have to form your mouth into a kiss to sip from its lip. In this facial mode the wine is channelled directly to the tip of the tongue where the taste buds that recognize sweetness are located.

The French have to take some of the blame for legitimizing the coupe as the quintessential champagne glass. The cover of Patrick Forbes's seminal book, Champagne, *bears the photo of a piece of Sèvres porcelain moulded, it is said, from Marie-Antoinette's left breast. Charming though that may be, champagne tastes better out of clear glass than out of a china bra.*

In Arthur Koestler's novel Darkness at Noon *the hero, Rubashov, is imprisoned in a Russian jail for anti-Soviet activity. A prisoner in an adjoining cell establishes contact with him by tapping on the metal pipes. He is a White Russian officer who has been locked away for many years and he wants to know about the last woman Rubashov made love to. Rubashov, who had been more interested in the revolution, makes up a fantasy for him. At one point he says that her breasts would have fitted into champagne glasses.*

Koestler, I suspect, had in mind the saucer-shaped glass and not the ideal receptacle for champagne, the elongated flute.

I made myself very unpopular with the Ontario wine industry in 1984 when the Champagne producers took seven Ontario wineries to court for using the term "Canadian Champagne" on their labels. I was called as an expert witness on behalf of the French, who eventually lost the case. The judge ruled that they had waited too long to bring the action and that nobody could mistake a Canadian champagne for the genuine article. Perhaps that was true then, but Château des Charmes in Ontario does a pretty good imitation these days and so do Blue Mountain and Summerhill out in British Columbia.

The first time I ever tasted "Canadian Champagne" was at a Canada Day celebration in London in 1975. I was seated next to a British diplomat who took one sip of the Chateau-Gai sparkler and sniffed: "Fit only for launching enemy submarines."

In the European Community, not only is champagne protected as an appellation but the expression *méthode champenoise* is too. Only the Champenois can use the terms on their labels. Sparkling wines from Alsace, the Loire, Limoux, etc. have to call their wines made by the same bottle-fermented method, *vins mousseux*.

nobody could mistake a Canadian champagne for the genuine article

The Spanish were actually sued by the French in the 1960s over the use of "champagne" and when they lost they invented a name for their indigenous bubblies produced by the traditional method in San Sadurni de Noya. They called them *cava*. It was the giant Spanish sparkling wine producer Perelada that was the target of French anger. One of the expert witnesses on behalf of the French was the late English gastronome, Raymond Postgate, who was challenged by Perelada's lawyers as wanting "to reserve the word champagne only for the most expensive champagne, so that only the rich can enjoy champagne." To his everlasting credit Postgate replied, "What your clients want to do is to call margarine butter so that the poor can enjoy butter."

*T*here are some wine lovers, and I am one of them, who enjoy the taste of very old champagne. It has a slightly maderized, winey taste and prickles on the tongue rather than foaming. *The French, who generally like to drink their wines young, refer to this as le gout anglais (anything the French consider weird they ascribe to the English).*

My friend Stephen Kaplan in Chicago held a tasting this year (1997) of ten Veuve Clicquot champagnes from 1989 back to 1923. Most were served from magnums, apart from vintages 1942, 1928 and 1923. The latter had a coppery gold colour and a nose of biscuits, toast and baked apples. It was mellow on the palate with the nuttiness of an old Meursault. A remarkable wine for its age.

Michael Broadbent was also at that tasting; as a veteran auctioneer and a man who has probably tasted more great wines than anyone else on this planet, he passed on two tips that lovers of old champagne should know about: the first is that ullage (the air gap between the level of the wine and the business end of the cork) is not as dangerous in champagne as it is in still wines. A large air gap in a still wine could mean oxidation. In champagne that head space is taken up with carbon dioxide which has escaped from the wine and acts as a protective layer of gas to exclude oxygen.

The second recommendation Broadbent had was how to "refresh" old champagne.

The trick is to open a young non-vintage champagne along with the old bottle and pour into the glass a third to half of new wine before you pour the venerable bottle. According to Broadbent, the old wine will give the new wine character and the new wine will give the old wine life.

Veuve Clicquot's US president, Mireille Guiliano, was also at the tasting and she had this advice:

"Drinking from magnums is the ultimate way to drink cham-

pagne. Champagne is the wine of love and a magnum is the perfect size for two."

My kind of woman.

In the 1980s Robert Gourdin was Moët & Chandon's roving ambassador, based in New York. He had two party tricks that involved champagne: creating a champagne fountain and sabering the bottle.

The concept of sabering champagne bottles originated during the Napoleonic wars. Victorious French generals, hot from the battlefield, impatient for a celebratory glass of bubbly, had no time to remove the foil and untwist the wire muzzle. So they used their swords. The technique was described to me by Eugene Wagner, former General Manager of Toronto's Four Seasons Hotel. (You should not try this at home unless you are prepared to wear hockey gloves and a fencing mask as I did when I demonstrated the art to Arthur Black on his CBC radio programme, "Basic Black" a few years ago.)

According to Wagner, "You can use any kind of kitchen knife but it's better to have something that's heavy and with an edge to it. You take the paper off the neck of the bottle and untwist the metal wire. Then with an easy motion you slide the knife up the side of the bottle making sure the bottle is facing nobody. The blade will strike just under the lip of the bottle."

Champagne is under 90 pounds per square inch of pressure. The weakest part of the bottle is along the line of the seam of the bottle at the neck where the glass is thinnest. The resonance of the blow sends shock waves through the glass which triggers an explosion of gas. The sudden pressure breaks off the neck with the cork still in it. The cut is a clean one with no splinters getting into the wine. Needless to say you always lose some champagne.

Eugene Wagner is a member of the Confrérie du Sabre d'Or, an organization that came into existence in 1986, "to define the true art of sabering champagne"; in fact, he is the Connétable de la Region of Ontario and founder of the local Toronto chapter. The Metropolitan Hotel's Hemispheres restaurants and Mövenpick are currently the two caveaux where you can "discover the enchantingly pretentious Confrérie du Sabre d'Or."

The organization's founding chapter is in Vancouver, started by Philippe Pradel. Currently sabering there is performed at The Hermitage, The Five Sails, The Empress Room and Chez Thierry.

The Confrérie originated, of course, in Champagne to promote the sale of their product in restaurants. To this end its members try to develop chapters all over the world. Their mission statement, written by Prince Alain de Polignac, states, "The enchantment of wine has turned the warrior's gesture into an expression of joy. And what wine is more fitting than Champagne to fulfil this mission, the wine whose origin and image remain a perpetual contradiction...?"

The Confrérie put out a glossy magazine to celebrate its 10th anniversary. It was full of pictures of men in green capes and green hats that look like Robin Hood gone Country & Western. They also produce a pocket guide to the fifty-six restaurants throughout Europe whose owners or sommeliers will open your champagne with a saber.

The weapon itself was developed by the Confrérie: a short curved saber measuring about 80 centimeters in length with a gilded handle. It comes in a large felt covered box, the kind that duellists might have opened at dawn in a misty field. The Grande Maître of the Confrérie, Jean-Claude Jalloux, is shown in the anniversary magazine in comic-book form, instructing would-be sabreurs in the gentle art: *"Choisir une bouteille de Champagne bien fraiche...Invitez vos amis a s'éloigner de la trajectoire du bouchon...."*

But back to Robert Gourdin, the first man I ever saw sabering champagne. He came to Toronto in 1982 to promote Moët & Chandon at a press conference in a downtown hotel.

The invitation to the wine writers stated that he would recreate the famous Moët wine fountain using Baccarat crystal glasses and he would also demonstrate the lost art of sabering the champagne. Intrigued, a jaded press corps turned out in force, including two television news crews. The event was held in a hotel ballroom in the centre of which was a magnificent "fountain," over a metre and a half high, of Baccarat glasses arranged in a cone shape with a single champagne glass at the top.

...he would recreate the famous Moët wine fountain...

I had seen the fountain effect performed spectacularly in Reims a couple of years earlier. The idea is to pour champagne into the head glass which is set in such a way that the overflow spills into the tier of glasses below. It's rather like a solera effect. If you keep pouring champagne, eventually the cascading wine will fill all the glasses which are then dismantled one by one from the top and handed around to the assembled company (all of whom get sticky fingers). Needless to say it takes about a couple of cases of wine to create — not an event for the frugal nineties.

On this occasion Robert Gourdin decided that he would show his prowess with the saber and then end the spectacle with the fountain. Showman that he was, Gourdin advised his audience to stand well back as he held the champagne bottle in one hand and waved the short sword in the other. The TV cameramen moved in to record the moment.

With a deft flick of the wrist Gourdin slid the blade up the bottle. There was a small bang and the cork, still encased in an inch of glass, went flying across the room. It struck the conical pile of Baccarat crystal in the centre like a mortar shell and brought the whole thing down in a shower of broken glass.

A CHTO-TV camerman, who had just returned unscathed

from a two-week assignment in Beirut, covering the Lebanese war, was hit by a shard of flying glass and cut across the nose.

Monsieur Gourdin could open twenty-four bottles of champagne in five minutes, although he bears a scar with fourteen stitches on his right wrist as a testimony to the danger of the enterprise.

*W*hen I told my son Guy about sabering champagne, he informed me that his contemporaries use the same technique on beer bottles. And much to my chagrin he showed me how they do it. I made him promise not to do it again, citing the danger of flying glass.

Guy also showed me a trick his peers use to stop a shaken-up beer from overflowing the glass. If you rub your forefinger down the side of your nose and plunge it into the head, like Moses parting the Red Sea, the foam will subside. I can't explain the physics but it has something to do with the oil of your skin and its effect on effervescence. It sounds disgusting and something one would not do at a dinner party, but my son assures me that it would, no doubt, work with champagne too.

A friend of mine, an accomplished amateur pianist, once told me that 60 per cent of our enjoyment of music is familiarity. If we can recognize the piece we secretly congratulate ourselves and identify more closely with the music and its interpreter. The psychological enjoyment of the work becomes more important than our critical judgement of it. By the same token I would say that 60 per cent of the enjoyment of wine is also psychological.

Our appreciation of wine, I contend, has more to do with mood, ambience and timing than it does with the intrinsic quality of the bottle on the table. Let me give you two examples: you are invited to dinner at the home of your bank manager. He has opened a bottle of Château Latour 1961. Just as you raise the glass to your lips he tells you he has to foreclose on your mortgage. That wine will taste like bilge water and the memory of the occasion will forever detract from your future enjoyment of Latour '61.

By the same token, if you are having a picnic with someone you love and you share a bottle of simple Beaujolais chilled in a stream it can taste like the nectar of the gods.

I visited the village of St. Emilion for the first time in 1966. I had an introduction to an English wine broker in Bordeaux, William Bolter. He was entertaining two American clients and he had suggested we have lunch in a restaurant whose name I have forgotten. It was off the main square on the hill, looking down on the tiled rooftops and winding streets. We ate outdoors; the sun was shining. It was an idyllic setting. The mâitre d' went into such extravagant praise of the proprietor's St. Emilion house wine from the 1964 vintage that we decided to try a bottle. It arrived at the table in a green bottle with no label or cork and did indeed taste wonderful as we basked in the July sunshine with our plate of cold cuts and cheeses. So much so that I decided I would purchase a bottle to take back to London with me to remember that convivial occasion.

The following February, on a rainy, cold London day, under skies the colour of pewter, I opened the bottle to recall that bright day, hoping for Proust's madeleine in vinous form.

The wine tasted terrible and I poured it down the sink. It wasn't corked; it wasn't oxidized; it just tasted bland. Bordeaux reds, like teenagers, do go through stages and perhaps this one had entered into its dumb phase from which it would awaken in a year or two, but it was a monumental disappointment.

Sometimes I'm asked what is the finest bottle of wine I have ever tasted. I can answer this question unequivocably: it was a red Burgundy, Musigny 1964 Comte de Vogüé. I opened it on February 13, 1975, the night my son Guy was born. No other Burgundy has tasted like it since and I must confess I consumed the whole bottle myself. But then, I was psychologically primed to receive a great wine.

Cabernet Sauvignon

> *"The English mistake love of claret for emotion."*
>
> JANE AUSTEN

*T*he licence plate of my car reads CLARET which, I suppose, tells you that my heart is in Bordeaux. Perhaps because I was immersed in these wines when I started my interest in the subject.

My finest wine drinking experiences have been with Burgundy, both red and white; but for sheer consistency and dependability red Bordeaux can't be beaten.

When you spend $75 for a second growth red Bordeaux of a good year you can almost bank on the fact that it will be worth the money. Unfortunately, you can't say the same about Burgundy. The reason has a lot to do with French inheritance laws. When a vineyard owner dies his estate must be divided among his heirs. This has caused the fragmentation of Burgundy vineyards over the years. Take one of Burgundy's most famous properties, Clos de Vougeot, for instance. This walled Grand Cru vineyard, south of the village of Vougeot with its imposing château set among the vines, occupies 125 acres (the same size as Château Ducru-Beaucaillou in Bordeaux's St. Julien commune). Of the 77 growers or négociants who own parcels of the Clos, 23 have establishments only large enough to produce a mere three barrels of wine a year. Legally each owner, however small his or her allotment of vines, could produce a wine bearing the Clos de Vougeot label but many sell their wines to brokers; still, there are dozens of products from this single vineyard labelled as Clos de Vougeot — wines that vary not only because of the quality of the grapes (the lower part of the sloping vineyard by the road is not as good as the upper part around the château) but also because the individual winemaking styles vary. Hence, the minefield for the prospective purchaser.

In Burgundy, the reputation of the shipper or the grower takes precedence over the geographical location of the vineyard.

In Bordeaux, by contrast, the name of the château branded on the cork is your guarantee that the wine comes from a single, autonomous property, made with one winemaking philosophy and bottled on the premises (*mis en bouteille au château*).

I first visited Bordeaux in 1966 with my friend Arnold Seltzer, in his old Jaguar. We drove from London, took the ferry from Dover to Calais and proceeded south to Paris, through Chartres with its magnificent cathedral and along the Loire Valley, driving as far west as Azay-le-Rideau. Then we cut south through Charentes to Bordeaux city.

My wine-importer friend Lionel Frumkin, who had set me up with the Bordeaux cellar, had arranged for us to visit several of the châteaux his company dealt with.

Peter Sichel gave us a tour of Château Palmer. On the top floor of the magnificent building we saw the rooms where German soldiers had been billeted during the war. There were still graffiti on the walls and the old iron bedsteads in rows. It reminded me of the dormitory I slept in at Epsom College, a minor English public school set on the downs near the race course where the Derby is run. On Derby Day the boys were forbidden to attend the race for fear, no doubt, that the presence of bookies in checkered jackets and their fidgety touts might turn us impressionable teenagers into hopeless gamblers. Needless to say, there were illicit books kept by the more enterprising students.

young Cabernet Sauvignon ... tastes like green peppers infused in cold, strong tea.

I cannot say that I enjoyed what I tasted out of the barrel when we were invited into the cellars. I was a neophyte and young Cabernet Sauvignon is no fun. Tannic and hard, it tastes like green peppers infused in cold, strong tea. And the 1965 vintage, the current wine in barrel at that time, was one of the worst in the history of winemaking. The wines of that year, according to Michael Broadbent in his *Great Vintage Book*, ranged "from insignificant to execrable."

Other vintages that fall into the same category are 1951 and 1968. If you had the misfortune to have been born in any one of these years, may I offer you a piece of advice. When you visit a Bordeaux château, or any other French wine region for that matter, and the winemaker asks you the year of your birth, lie through your teeth. Say you were born in 1928, 1945, 1947, 1961, 1970 or 1982 — whatever you can get away with. (Any younger and you shouldn't be drinking anyway.)

According to the Universal Winemakers' Lexicon — the secret knowledge known only to those who spend most of their life underground in cellars — there is no such thing as a bad vintage. There are "difficult" vintages, "challenging" vintages and "useful" vintages, but no bad vintages. Only diplomats and James Joyce scholars can understand the nuances of these euphemisms.

"Difficult" actually means catastrophic: "We had howling gales and frigid temperatures during harvesting and alien spaceships did the crush in the vineyard when they tried to land." "Challenging" means, "What the hell are we going to do with grapes so green they make lemon juice taste sweet?" "Useful" means, "It's a mediocre vintage which we have to sell anyway and since it has no ageing potential we'll tell the restaurants they can put it on their lists and pretend it's ready for drinking now."

Even more bizarre are the contortions that winemakers go through when they compile vintage reports. These are documents that they send around to wine merchants and the wine press giving their assessment of the quality of the grape crop and the potential quality of the wine they will make from it. Somehow in these documents, the treachery of the weather gods is thwarted at the last moment and the harvest turns out to be much better than anticipated.

To listen to wine growers talk, every vintage is sensational unless it is patently obvious to the wine-buying public that the previous six months were a living hell of tempest, tornado and earthquake. If you read the annual vintage reports the world over you soon detect the note of frenzied optimism that characterizes them all.

... Ark Wines predicts a small but good quality crop...

The vintage projection for the year of Noah's flood probably read: "Early prospects for an abundant harvest have been revised because of unseasonal rainfall in the Mount Ararat region. However, with the appearance of a rainbow and some late summer sunshine, Ark Wines predicts a small but good quality crop once the snorkellers have gathered it in."

I think Château Beychevelle must have been embarrassed by their 1965s because on leaving, Arnold Seltzer and I were presented with a half bottle of their 1964 vintage. The winemaker explained that the wine was very forward and would mature faster in a half bottle than in a full bottle.

This was good news for Arnold and me because we planned to drink it as soon as we found a restaurant where you could bring your own bottle.

Our ultimate destination was the house we had rented for a week in Valbonne, a village in the hills above Cannes. The house belonged to a friend from my time at Trinity College, Dublin. As we left Bordeaux to drive south through Carcassone, Narbonne and Beziers and drop to the coast at Sète, Arnold's ancient Jaguar began to show signs of feeling the strain. It began coughing and wheezing and threatened to die.

Finding a Jaguar dealer in Languedoc-Roussillon is not the easiest thing in the world. The garage where we stopped diagnosed the problem as a faulty fuel pump, and suggested that we limp into Marseilles and have it fixed.

The shortest and fastest way to Marseilles was via the autoroute. The mechanic told us the only way that we could guarantee that the car did not break down on this busy highway was to keep hitting the fuel pump with a rubber mallet to maintain the flow of petrol to the engine.

Since it was Arnold's car I was handed the mallet. The fuel pump was located in the trunk of the car, so we took the baggage out of the trunk and put it on the back seat. I climbed into the trunk and held on with my right hand as I struck the fuel pump with the mallet in my left.

Concerned that I might fall out, Arnold halved his habitual speed of 100 m.p.h. to fifty.

Things were going along well under the circumstances. The Jaguar seemed to be responding to having its fuel pump tattooed with a rubber mallet. Cars and trucks were whizzing by us and God knows what they must have thought seeing a man in an open trunk bashing the interior with a mallet. From the licence plate they could tell we were from England which, for the French, would be explanation enough.

And then we arrived at the toll booth.

Arnold eased the car up to the attendant and handed him the ticket.

"The chap in the back will pay," he said, in French.

The attendant, one of those Frenchmen you usually see riding bicycles with baguettes tied to the pillion, craned his neck, searching past the luggage on the back seat for a passenger.

"But, monsieur, there is no one there!"

Arnold inched the car forward and a hand emerged from the trunk holding a 100 franc note.

In my best French I said: "I always travel this way. I get car sick."

We found our restaurant: a small, seven-room inn called Le Cheval Blanc on the outskirts of Valbonne. The chef was German and the food was amazing. It was the only place mentioned under Valbonne in the *Michelin Guide*, where it had a crossed spoon and fork, symbolizing "plain but good."

Valbonne was a village that Hollywood might have picked as the location for a French comedy of manners. It had the typical bakery and general store, and little else. In the square as you entered the main street was a small fountain.

Our first night, a Saturday, Arnold and I ate at Le Cheval Blanc. I don't recall what we ate on that occasion, but I know we were so impressed that we asked to meet the chef. He came out of the kitchen in his food, stained whites, wiping his hands on a towel. He was a small dark man whose face fairly lit up when we expressed our appreciation for his food. He apologized that his menu was not extensive but if we were to come back on the following Tuesday for dinner he would cook whatever dishes we wished.

"How about *truites aux amandes?*" said Arnold.

"And *coq au vin*," I said.

It was agreed. We would return at eight the following Tuesday evening for the specially prepared meal. Arnold would have the trout in almonds and I the chicken cooked in red wine.

Tuesday morning we noticed two fish swimming in the fountain that had not been there before. It turned out that these were the trout *sans amandes*.

> *Tuesday morning we noticed two fish swimming in the fountain...*

While I eat everything that is put in front of me — except for Birds' Eye custard — I feel rather squeamish about the sight of my prospective meal "on the hoof," as it were. Knowing I am about to devour something that is healthy and alive makes me project in the cinema of the mind its imminent execution in the kitchen. I have never been able to select "my" lobster from a tank, and the sight of those trout swimming lazily in circles under the azure skies of Provence made me feel somewhat ambivalent about the evening's gastronomic adventure.

There was no one else in Le Cheval Blanc's dining room when we arrived — which is probably why the chef had invited us back on a Tuesday night. We brought along with us our half bottle of Beychelle 1964 to have with our cheese. The chef greeted us at the door, relieved us of the bottle and suggested we have an aperitif at the bar while we studied the wine list for our first course.

We had a Lillet on the rocks and ordered a half carafe of Bandol Blanc and a half carafe of Bandol Rouge, the house wines.

I was hoping there might be a Sancerre or a Chablis on the list, but the selection extended only as far north as the Rhône. In fact, there is nothing quite as chauvinistic as a French wine list: in Bordeaux you won't find any Burgundies; in Burgundy don't look for Côte-Rôtie or Hermitage; in Alsace you're more likely to find the wines of California and Australia than anything from the Loire!

It is not that the wines of other regions do not exist, merely that they cannot possibly be as good as those that grow within walking distance of the restaurant. (For years the reverse psychology has applied to Canadian wines. Anything that bore an imported label had to be better than the local article. You were lucky if you could find an Ontario wine on a Toronto wine list.)

Arnold and I were invited to sit at the table when the chef had prepared the first course. No sooner had the wine been poured than the dish arrived: two steaming, plump trout smothered in slivered almonds and beurre blanc.

I thought it strange that we were not offered a menu to choose a first course, but seeing the size of Arnold's dish it was obvious that a first course would not be necessary. Then two plates arrived and the waitress deftly cut the fish lengthwise in two and transferred a portion of trout with a spoon and fork onto each.

Arnold and I looked at each other. We had ordered two main dishes. The trout in front of us heaped with grilled almonds was the size of a small convertible.

It was perfectly cooked. The fish fell away from the bone. The sweetness of the butter, the crunch of the almonds and the hint of parsley set off the taste of the trout. Each mouthful was a benediction for the palate.

We could have ended the meal there and been satisfied, but then the coq au vin arrived in a huge earthenware pot. The waitress placed it on the table between us and lifted the lid. The fragrance of wine and chicken, of morels and lardons of bacon, of pearl onions and garlic and *herbes de Provence* filled the room.

> **I had never tasted chicken like that before in my life.**

The waitress began ladling huge portions onto two fresh plates.

I had never tasted chicken like that before in my life. The spicing was perfection, the meat moist and succulent, lifted by the flavour of red wine and a splash of brandy. The fleshiness of the tiny onions, the saltiness of the lardons and the earthy flavor of the spongy morels made a wonderful counterpoint to the buttery softness of the chicken. (I'm beginning to sound like a food writer, for God's sake!)

It occurred to me that several birds must have gone into the pot as there were at least six legs that I counted. The chef, however, swore that it was one chicken. I was only thankful that I had not met it scratching around the village.

There are two stages in an oenophile's life. The first is the discovery of wine; the second, the revelation of *fine* wine.

Think back to the very first glass of wine you drank. Not the one your parents allowed you to drink at Christmas, suitably watered, as a special treat in your pre-teens, but the one that made the leap from Coca-Cola and other sweet carbonated drinks to beverage alcohol. Ten to one it was Mateus Rosé or Baby Duck.

If you're Jewish it was probably Manischewitz or Mogen David, those tooth-rattlingly sweet Concord wines that graced the Passover table and filled the silver cup on Friday nights to bless the arrival of the Sabbath.

My parents kept no wine in the house, save a bottle of Manischewitz that lasted them about six months. My stepfather drank no alcohol except on ceremonial or sacramental occasions. When I would visit them in Montreal he would say to my mother, "Mimi, bring out the wine."

The wine would be the heel of a bottle of Manischewitz that my mother, for reasons best known to herself, kept secreted in the linen closet which was warm — a technique used in Madeira to "bake" wine, only they do it in barrels under the roof.

"That's fine," I would say as my mother poured a brimming measure of the browning, lukewarm stuff into a wine glass so thin you would think it would burst like a bubble when you put it to your lips.

My Uncle Louis, on the other hand, loved fine wine. At his table I was initiated into the mysteries of top-flight Bordeaux and Burgundy. Particularly Bordeaux, which he favoured above all other wines. Uncle Louis lived in London on a street that looked like a winding country lane called *Crooked Usage*, in an impressive brick house . He was a wealthy man who enjoyed the good things of life, especially the pleasures of the table. He and my Aunt Helen were forever travelling, via Switzerland, to destinations around the world. He once had an interest in a whisky distillery.

Uncle Louis was a vegetarian until the sun went down. He used to take me to lunch at an Italian fish restaurant near his office in Fitzroy Square. The only wine he ever ordered there was Soave Bolla. But in his own home it was First Growth Bordeaux and the best domaine-bottled Burgundies.

Usually I dined there on a Friday night with other members of the family. Uncle Louis was the oldest son in a family of two boys and six girls, of whom my mother was the youngest. I was the youngest of his seventeen nephews and nieces.

Uncle Louis would sit at one end of the table and Aunty Helen at the other. Invariably there were twelve people and sufficient wine to ensure that the glasses were never empty.

I remember first tasting Château Lafite 1959 at his table. I didn't like it. I said that it tasted like melted pencil leads.

I said that it tasted like melted pencil leads.

"That's what it's meant to taste like!" roared Uncle Louis.

He was famous for talking to everybody and would embarrass his nieces and nephews when he took us out to restaurants by speaking to waiters in a cockney accent. I don't know why he did this, but I suspect it was a bizarre display of democracy, as if he were saying to the waiter, "I might be rich and able to dine here but underneath I'm just like you." The waiters didn't appreciate it.

Once he mortified a female cousin by leaning over to a neighbouring table and pulling their bottle from the ice bucket. He studied the label over his rimless glasses and replaced the bottle, muttering, "Inferior vintage."

Towards the end of his life he confided to me that he was buying his wine in half bottles. Aunty Helen did not drink any more and a bottle was too much for him. I used to recommend wines to him that I had bought at auction, Third and Fourth Growth clarets of great quality for the price. But he would shake his head and say, "Nah, nah, with First Growths I know where I stand."

He was, in retrospect, a wine snob, my Uncle Louis, but he was a great character and is sorely missed. Everybody should have an Uncle Louis.

My own father, a doctor, did not care for wine. I can't remember ever seeing a bottle in our house at Herne Hill in London. He drank whisky and water, gin and orange (which I would mix for him when he came home from evening surgery) and at lunch, beer. The beer came in large brown bottles with stone stoppers. He drank it out of a half-pint pewter tankard with a glass bottom — a golf trophy he had won. (He was an 8-handicap golfer and I was a golf orphan.)

My father's practice stretched from Kennington to Lambeth (including Lambeth Walk) and several of his patients had council flats overlooking the Oval cricket ground. I remember in the late 1940s watching Test matches from their windows. I saw the legendary Australian batsman Sir Don Bradman play and the great English openers, Len Hutton, Cyril Washbrook and Dennis Compton would come in at first wicket down. The latter was the first sportsman I remember who advertised a product: he was Britain's Brylcreem boy.

Another of my father's patients was a chef who worked at a fashionable Piccadilly restaurant called Hatchett's. He used to make my birthday cakes, which I could never eat because they were heavy with cream and spiked with rum, not to the taste of an eleven-year-old boy. Before the National Health Service was introduced, my father and I used to dine a lot at Hatchett's — probably because the chef couldn't pay his doctor's bills.

In an attempt to turn me into a doctor, my father sent me to Epsom College in Surrey where the sons of doctors went. Our nearest rival was Leatherhead School where the sons of clergymen were sent, no doubt to turn them into clerics.

The food at English public schools was (and doubtless still is) notoriously bad. Even at that age I recognized this fact. How bad? Well, I once took the train from Epsom to Victoria Station in London just to eat the hot-dogs they served in the buffet on the platform.

Epsom College's most famous old boy was also its most notorious. Stewart Grainger, the English matinee idol of the forties and fifties, was asked to leave the college for unspecified crimes and misdemeanours. He returned one Open Day, at the height of his film stardom, to watch a rugby match with Jean Simmons on his arm; no doubt to show the masters who had despaired of him that he had made his way in the world notwithstanding his public school education.

I nearly suffered a similar fate over a bottle of wine: it was at Epsom that I had my first taste of Sauternes. I was thirteen years old.

On the wall of the school gym in a glass frame was the Latin dictum *Mens sana in corpore sano*. In pursuit of the second part of that dictum, all members of the school had to take daily exercise: rugby in winter and cricket in summer. On days when there were no organized games we had to run two different triangles outside the school grounds — the Fir Tree Triangle and the Long Triangle, which were, if memory serves, a mile and a half and two and a half miles, respectively. On Sundays we had to go for a walk on the Downs.

While I enjoyed watching cricket, I was not very good at it. The less good one was at it, the further one was placed from the action. I was positioned in the outfield. Since there were some 500 boys at Epsom, there were numerous games in progress at the same time, too many for the masters to monitor. And being juniors, my peers and I were relegated to the farthest cricket pitch, well out of sight of prefects and other watchdogs.

My friend Richard Ivor, also an outfielder, and I had contrived on our run the day before to slip into an off-licence and buy a bottle of B&G Sauternes which we smuggled back into my locker. There was no particular reason for the selection of a dessert wine. The bottle happened to be nearest to the door, and the wine was priced much lower than the reds or dry whites in view.

Richard had a Swiss Army knife with a corkscrew. We smuggled the bottle onto the cricket pitch and while the play was in action we settled down in the long grass on the boundary at approximately square leg and passed the Sauternes between us. Since we had no glasses we swigged straight from the bottle. In the sunshine the warm sweet wine soon took its toll.

We staggered back to our house and our general demeanour was duly noted by the prefects who were alerted to our inebriated state when we both fell asleep over our books during prep. Hungover and abject with contrition, Richard Ivor and I were summoned before the housemaster who soon got to the bottom of the matter. What had induced our current state? Where had we acquired the prohibited alcohol? How had we manage to smuggle it onto the cricket field? What was the vintage?

...we swigged straight from the bottle. In the sunshine the warm sweet wine soon took its toll.

We expected to be expelled for our crime, which made our condition even worse.

The housemaster, "Nifty" Colyer, delivered six of the best. As I left his study rubbing my rear, he said, "By the way, if you insist on drinking Sauternes, be sure to chill it next time."

*T*he oldest claret I have ever had the pleasure of tasting was a Château Lafite 1865. I bought it from an American friend, Ray Smart, who had bid £108 for a lot of six bottles at a Christie's auction in London in 1969. I hate to think what that bottle would cost today! Like its sister vintage 1864, the 1865 was a five-star year. The mouth-blown bottle had no label apart from a neck tag that proclaimed its provenance as Château Lafite. The fill was high shoulder.

The question was, whom was I going to share this treasure with? I invited Gordon Bucklitsch, who was working at Grant's of St. James's at the time, his assistant John McCluskey, and another member of the firm whose name escapes me now. The three of them arrived at my London flat late one morning. Knowing that the wine would begin to oxidize rapidly as soon as the cork was pulled, we decided that we would not decant the wine. We would pour it quickly and drink it immediately.

I entrusted the uncorking to Gordon. The cork came away perfectly. There was a little bottle stink of the stale air at the head of the neck but when this dissipated, the bouquet of leather, truffles, tobacco and red berries began to fill the room. The colour as it poured was a deep rosé. The taste was silky and sweet and lingered hauntingly on the palate. It was a magnificent wine.

We just sat there smiling at each other as we sipped this 104-year old wine.

And then it began to turn. About twenty minutes after it was opened the wine began to taste like balsamic vinegar.

The only way I can describe the experience is that it was like watching a beautiful old dowager enter a room. She is dressed in her best ball gown, and adorned with ruby necklace and a tiara. She offers the room a magnificent smile — and drops dead.

I still carry the memory of that magnificent wine even though the mouth-blown bottle has long since disappeared.

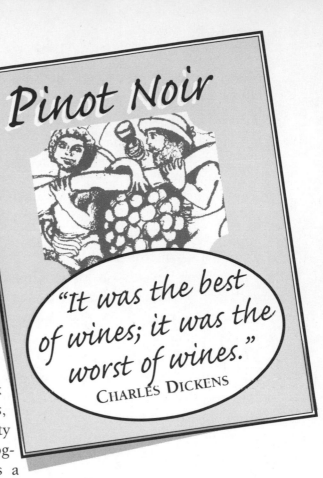

Pinot Noir

"It was the best of wines; it was the worst of wines."
CHARLES DICKENS

*A*ccording to Jancis Robinson in her seminal work *Vines, Grapes and Wines,* "The first specific variety of *vinifera* to be recognized and named was a Pinot in Burgundy in 1375." Now that's provenance.

Red Burgundy is an enigma. Just like the little girl with the curl: when it is good it is very, very good; but when it is bad it's horrid. Maybe that's why Pinot Noir is the winemaker's Holy Grail. Marq de Villiers entitled his insightful book on Pinot Noir *The Heartbreak Grape,* and every winegrower knows that this variety is the Bitch Goddess.

In Burgundy, Pinot Noir's natural home, it ripens maybe three times in ten years. In California and Oregon it ripens all the time, but invariably the flavours go over the top into jamminess.

There are very few Pinot Noirs — grown in Burgundy or anywhere else — that achieve that ethereal, silken taste that slips down the throat, as one Burgundian producer described it, like "Baby Jesus dressed in velvet trousers."

How to capture in prose that unique flavour which has the whiff of the barnyard overlaid with violets, the taste of raspberries and black cherries with nuances of rust, vanilla and tomato leaf? A contradiction perhaps, because who wants to drink a wine that smells of the stable and tastes like old pipes and plant life? Yet it works, and when it does there is no finer wine in the world.

The French and the English liken that fragrance of fine Burgundy to "shit." Both nations are more anal, or perhaps more honest and uninhibited, than North Americans. (The vignerons of Beaujolais, when pleased by the crush of their Gamay grapes, use the expression *ça pisse dru* which means, in sanitized translation, "the juice looks very concentrated.")

I have mentioned before that I grew up on claret but my finest wine experiences have been Burgundies.

Red Bordeaux enthusiasts are dog lovers at heart. They cherish loyalty and dependability. They are optimists, not used to disappointment. Red Burgundy aficionados, on the other hand, are cat lovers who have no expectations at all and are mildly surprised when their pet curls up in their lap purring. They are anticipating rebuff at every turn.

You have to have a touch of the cynic to pursue Pinot Noir through the bewildering maze of Côte d'Or shippers and estates.

Pinot Noir's schizophrenic nature was best summed up for me at the World Vinifera Conference in Seattle, Washington, in 1995. Alex Gambal, who works for the Burgundy shippers Becky Wasserman Selection, informed the assembled participants: "Burgundy is a minefield. You can be blown to hell or blown to heaven."

Trying to capture the nature and character of wine on paper is a wine writer's most difficult job. Since a grapevine has the life span of Biblical man (three score years and ten) and the grape is 80 per cent water, almost as much as a human being, wine is very human. Like us, it can catch cold. It doesn't like bright light, hates being shaken about or travelling great distances. It can live for 100 years but mostly dies younger. It has no sense of humour even when it's feeling good.

How then can we not talk about wine in human terms? Before the enfeeblement of the English language by the feminist movement, wines were described as either being masculine or feminine depending on their weight or finesse. The wines of Volnay were definitely feminine while those of Vosne-Romanée pumped iron.

I once described an Alsatian Gewürztraminer as a lumberjack wearing too much aftershave; a Californian Chardonnay was a Mohammed Ali of a wine that proclaimed itself as soon as its cork was drawn. Other wines were librarians who whispered at you or cheerleaders without depth.

> *... a Californian Chardonnay was a Mohammed Ali of a wine...*

This kind of vinous anthropomorphism once got me into trouble with the Maria Callas International Club. On March 20, 1993, I received the following letter from Jeanne Handzic, the club's founder, from Croydon, Surrey (a stone's throw from where I went to school at Epsom).

Dear Mr. Aspler,

One of my Members in Toronto has kindly drawn your recent article to my attention, namely "'91 Was A Red-Letter Year" in the 13th March 1993 edition of The Toronto Star.

I readily admit that I am far from being a wine expert so also admit that I cannot quite discern your various comments on wine and their vintages.

However, where MARIA CALLAS is concerned, maybe I do know a little more!

I wonder if you would be so kind as to put pen to paper and let me have an explanation of the relevance between "Pinot Noir" and Maria Callas? You would probably say "...if you knew or tasted "Pinot Noir," you would know." A fair comment, but I don't.

Were you intending the (to me at least) somewhat strange comparison between some grapes with one of the world's greatest opera singer of all times to be complimentary to the latter, or not?

Hoping I may hear from you, I remain meanwhile,

Yours sincerely...

I must confess I did not reply to this letter. I could not for the life of me begin to explain to Ms Handzic, the keeper of the flame of the Maria Callas shrine, that what I wrote in no way trivialized the soprano's reputation or accomplishments. By my lights, calling Pinot Noir "the Maria Callas of grapes" was the supreme compliment to both parties.

O f all Pinot Noir grown outside the Côte d'Or, Oregon comes closest to the Burgundian model; and it's no coincidence that Burgundy shipper Robert Drouhin's daughter Veronique makes what I consider to be one of the best Oregon Pinot Noirs at Domaine Drouhin in the Dundee Hills.

Too many New World winemakers try to reinvent the wheel; they strain for effect by using too much oak and too much alcohol. In baseball terms, they hit for power rather than batting for average and as a result they strike out too often. Eventually they come to realize that the big, bruising wines (Chardonnays that whack you over the head with a two by four or Zinfandels that take you out with the best of three falls) are not fun to drink. Elegance and finesse are what the best wines are about.

Early in my career as a wine writer, Bruno Prats, the proprietor of Cos d'Estournel, told me something that I have never forgotten. The Bordelais and the French nation as a whole were in mourning following English wine merchant Steven Spurrier's Paris happening in 1976 when he held a blind tasting of California Cabernet Sauvignon pitted against First and Second Growth clarets. The tasters were French, and to their collective chagrin the Californians carried the day. This was the first real challenge to the supremacy of French wines since Mendes France tried to get his countrymen to drink milk.

> *Elegance and finesse are what the best wines are about.*

Certainly there were a few Californian Cabernets that could challenge the top flight red Bordeaux in 1976, but only a few, and there is a natural tendency to believe that these superior wines represented the standard of the industry at that time. They did not, although today there are more drinkable California Cabs than there are red Bordeaux in the price range where most of us shop.

Since Spurrier, the Oedipean game of blind tasting against the French model has become a national sport in the United States and Australia. The French can take cold comfort from the fact they are the yardstick of excellence against which every vintner with a steel tank and a 225-litre barrique measures his or her progress.

Invariably, in such blind tasting contests, the French lose out. It is a documented phenomenon that highly extractive, jammy Cabernets with a fleshy mouth-feel and a zap of new oak will triumph over the discreet, complex, harmonious wines of the

Médoc, Graves, St. Émilion and Pomerol.

But, asks Bruno Prats rhetorically, what would you rather drink with your rack of lamb? A fat, fruity California Cab that bores you after the first glass or an elegant claret that refreshes the palate and does not overpower the flavour of the dish?

Travelling by car through Burgundy is like running your eye down a great wine list. The resonating names are cheek by jowl. Chassagne-Montrachet, Puligny-Montrachet, Meursault, Monthélie, Volnay, Pommard, Beaune, Savigny, Aloxe-Corton, Pernand-Vergelesses, Nuits St. Georges, Vosne-Romanée, Vougeot, Morey-St.-Denis, Gevrey-Chambertin. Unpretentious villages, a place of farmers, unlike the self-conscious grandeur of Bordeaux with its turreted châteaux and the Mercedes parked out front. But the land here in Burgundy is the most expensive agricultural real estate on earth.

And then there is Beaune, the ancient walled city under whose narrow streets lies a labyrinth of tunnels where shippers store their wines. Cobbled streets with tightly-packed houses whose steep roofs are decorated with coloured slates set in diamond patterns. I once cycled from Villié-Morgon in Beaujolais, up through the Mâconnais and the Côte de Beaune to the city of Beaune during harvest time. The pickers waved and threw bunches of Pinot Noir the size of pine cones at our group as we passed. There is no better way to see wine country than from the saddle of a bike. Protected by a windshield you miss the smells and the connection with the terroir.

I have had the pleasure of visiting Burgundy many times (at Geisweiller I once had a 1927 for lunch which was miraculous), but the best time I ever had was when a group of executives from Commonwealth Holiday Inns spent the day with the Burgundy négociant, Roland Remoissenet.

It began with a tour of his office and cellars built into the old city walls of Beaune. Roland is an accomplished chef and enjoys entertaining his guests to lunch which he cooks himself in the small kitchen hung with copper pots next to his office. We ate off plates monogrammed with crossed flint-lock pistols from a restaurant named La Cartouche which I believe he once owned or in which he had an interest.

Apart from wielding a wooden spoon, Roland's other passion was the castle outside Beaune he had bought and lovingly restored. It was a real honest-to-God castle with battlements, a moat (dry), drawbridge and portcullis. He had spent a fortune restoring it to its original glory. When our party arrived we were greeted by a ceremonial trumpet fanfare.

The one thing that upset Roland was the presence of crows who fouled his battlements. The sight of them so incensed him that he would take up his .303 Lee Enfield rifle and take pot shots at them. One day he was visited by a neighbouring farmer who was in a highly agitated state. Twisting his hat in his hands, he enquired if "monsieur would be willing to purchase the cow he had shot."

In addition to his other talents, Roland Remoissenet is an artist. He restores and paints old musical instruments, such as the mechanical wind organ that plays with parchment scrolls. The brightly coloured contraption graces one end of the castle's main hall. In honour of our Canadian group's visit he had scoured Europe to get a parchment version of "O Canada" he could play on the machine. His agent found one in Venice.

In the dungeon below the hall of his castle Roland Remoissenet had recreated a Chamber of Horrors, fashioning out of papier-mâché life-size figures of tortured prisoners hanging from the walls in chains, complete with blood stains. I still have a photo of broadcaster Jeremy Brown with his hand on the dagger that has been plunged into the chest of one of the unfortunate occupants.

There is also a genuine skeleton in the dungeon. When we enquired whose it was he told us it was Japanese; Roland was very

> There is also a genuine skeleton in the dungeon.

disappointed that he could not find a French one, but M. Mitterand would not oblige.

After dinner in the main hall and copious quantities of Remoissenet wine, Roland disappeared and returned dressed like Napoleon.

He informed us that we all had to choose hats from a trunk in the corner. Inside was a selection of eighteenth and nineteenth century French headgear with ostrich feathers and rosettes. Our group was all male, the top brass of the Commonwealth Holiday Inn chain, and they were not accustomed to being part of the entertainment. But since we had all been sufficiently lubricated with Burgundy, we complied with our host's request and finished the meal wearing hats. He then played the wind organ which he himself accompanied on the drum.

Burgundians know how to have fun.

The first time I visited Burgundy I was driving with my friend Arnold Seltzer from London, in his old Jaguar. As I described earlier, we had already toured through the Loire and Bordeaux, stayed at Valbonne in the Alpes Maritimes, and were headed north on our way home. We found ourselves on a Sunday in a village just outside of Beaune, enchantingly named Bouze-lès-Beaune. French villages, when they are closed, look deserted. There was no one on the street, no open doors, nothing to say that the village was inhabited.

We cruised along the main road looking for *Vente* signs in the hopes that we might find a small vintner where we could taste and buy some wine. But we saw nothing.

Eventually we came across a man who was sawing logs on a wooden trestle at the side of the road. We stopped and I wound down the window.

"Excuse me, sir," I said, "but is there anywhere around here that we could taste some wine?"

The man put down his saw and wiped the sawdust from his sweating forehead.

"You're interested in wine?" he asked.

"Yes."

"Come with me."

We followed him into the gated property that rose from the roadside where he had been cutting wood. He led us up to a large house and invited us inside. We walked down some stone steps into the cellar. We found ourselves in a small *cave* with barrels, the kind that small négociants use to age the wines they have purchased.

Our host took a pipette and three glasses, offering us tastes from the barrels of his 1964 Burgundies.

We spent the whole afternoon in the cellar as he told us about each of the wines, how it would develop and why it was superior to the last. We were young kids with no connection to the wine trade other than a beginner's enthusiasm and a sense of awe. He had nothing to gain by impressing us with his wines or his knowledge; he was motivated solely by the generous and sharing nature that is so prevalent in the wine industry.

The man we had stumbled upon by the roadside that day was Michel Couvreur, a Burgundy négociant who shipped wines to The Windsor Arms Hotel and many of Toronto's clubs and restaurants until the 1980s.

Australia is beginning to make some very good Pinot Noir, especially in the Yarra Valley, an hour's drive northeast of Melbourne in the state of Victoria (referred to by the rest of the country as "Mexico" since it is the most southerly part of the country). Peach orchards and horse farms abound here, and mature rain forests of gum trees, black wattle and huge ferns that look like stunted palm trees.

Australia's leading wine writer, James Halliday, started a small winery near the endearingly-named town of Gruyere in 1985, called Coldstream Hills. His Pinot Noir Reserve is very Burgundian in style and really fine. In 1996 his operation was bought by the giant Southcorp who own Lindeman, Penfold's and Australia's most costly wine, Grange (the wine formerly known as Grange Hermitage).

On my most recent visit to Australia I was introduced to a small winery (one of twenty-one in the valley) which is mer-chandised by the BRL Hardy group about 15 kilometres away from Coldstream Hills as the cockatoo flies. It's called Yarra Burn and it gets its Pinot Noir from the Hoddles Creek vineyard.

The soil here is red volcanic and very fertile. With 55 inches of rain a year, vegetation has to be controlled with vigorous trimming.

The south-facing Pinot Noir block of Hoddles Creek,with a 28-degree slope, would make a great toboggan run. The fruit picked from this block goes into Yarra Burn's Bastard Hill label. (The hill was christened by the pickers. When they were asked to harvest that block one of them said, "Not that bastard hill again!")

On the drive back from lunch at Yarra Burn our host told us the story about the nearby Hazeldene resort, an exclusive, seven-room hotel with its own golf course and heli-pad. It also has its own dammed lake. The managing director of a large company wanted to hold a sales convention there. As an avid fisherman he asked if there were any trout in the lake. The secretary rang up the resort and enquired. "Yes, we have trout," came the reply — an answer that secured the reservation.

The owners immediately repaired to the local trout farm and purchased fifty large trout to stock the lake.

The first day the managing director took out his fly rod and cast away. He had a terrific time hauling in the trout one after the other. His final tally was forty-eight.

The conference was a great success. On leaving the resort, he signed the guest book, "Best damned trout fishing in Australia."

*I*n Adelaide I was threatened with a "pie floater." A pie floater is the Aussies' gastronomic equivalent of deep-fried Mars bars, much beloved in Glasgow where where they have yet to decide whether it is a main course or a dessert.

A pie floater is a meat pie that is set in a dish of green pea soup and then doused with tomato ketchup.

Apparently this delicacy is sold to late-night revellers, dispensed from wagons on street corners. No doubt so that the purveyors can make a quick escape.

While pie floaters are eaten in the early hours, that other Australian taste treat, Vegemite, is consumed with relish (which is what it is) at breakfast. Grown Australian men and women spread it thinly on bread or toast and recapture their childhood through its salty, yeasty taste.

I could not abide either Bovril or Marmite when I was growing up in England after the war; but Vegemite makes these meat and vegetable essences smell like ambrosia by comparison. The name Bovril comes from the Latin, bovis, meaning a cow or ox, and Bovril is, of course, beef extract. According to John Ayto in his A Gourmet's Guide, "During the 1930s and 1940s bovril was used as a euphemism for brothel ... and today the word is used colloquially in the waste-disposal trade for a ship which dumps sewage sludge in the open sea."

At the end of my visit to Australia, arranged by BRL Hardy, I wrote the following "Ode to Oz" by way of thanks.

> We're yet to see a kangaroo
> Or taste tartare of cockatoo
> But as your guests it is our right
> To shun the dreaded Vegemite.
> Oh brown and evil smelling spread
> What wine to serve? Rosé or red?
> Playboy, Cosmo, we seek advice —
> Sir James, you say, put one on ice.

And when it comes to meat pie floats
In green pea soup and ketchup coats
I think it's time to draw the line
And give up food for Hardy's wine.

The reference to "Sir James" is to Hardy's upmarket range of sparkling wines, named after the company's chairman, Sir James Hardy. The fruit comes from the Hoddles Creek vineyard, a blend of Pinot Noir and Chardonnay. The Prestige 1995 cuvée, with Pinot Noir from Tasmania, is the best Australian sparkling wine I have tasted.

Sir James Hardy inadvertently gave me a line I always use at wine tastings and one that never fails to raise a laugh. It shows how down-to-earth Australians are about their wines. In 1989 during my first trip to Chateau Reynella in McLaren Vale, the head office of the then Thomas Hardy & Sons, wine writers John Schreiner from Vancouver, Jacques Benoit from Montreal, Joel Butler (one of the very first American Masters of Wine) and I were invited to a tasting put on by James Hardy.

Hardy picked up a glass of red wine and said: "The way we tell the difference between a red and a white wine here in Australia is to hold up the glass like this. We put two fingers behind the glass like this, look through the glass and if you can see your fingers — it's a white wine."

Sauvignon Blanc

> "Sauvignon Blanc, my dear sir. It's nothing more than cat's pee on a gooseberry bush."
>
> CAPABILITY BROWN

Sauvignon Blanc is not a wine that immediately appeals to the neophyte wine drinker. It can have a green, grassy bouquet with an overtone of cat's tray. In cool climates, such as the Loire Valley, the flavour profile ranges from asparagus, green bean and peapod to gooseberry and elderberry. When it gets really ripe in warm years, such as 1995, more fig-like flavours are apparent.

In New Zealand, where Sauvignon Blanc has become a badge of honour since Cloudy Bay showed the world how good it can be, the taste is more towards passionfruit but with that nervous, racy acidity that freshens the mouth, cleanses the palate and does such marvellous things for goat's cheese.

I happen to love Sancerre and all those taut, tart little wines grown around Quincy and Menetou-Salon. I drink these wines whenever I can find them, which isn't often. On one trip to Paris in the mid-1980s I stopped by a wine bar called "Sancerre." If anyone would have Quincy they would, I reasoned, and sure enough they did.

The proprietor could have come out of Central Casting. He was a large man with a handlebar moustache waxed to needlepoints at both ends. He wore a none-too-clean apron and presided over the counter like a race horse owner lecturing a jockey. It was mid-afternoon and the place was quite full, considering that most people work at that time.

... a green, grassy bouquet with an overtone of cat's tray.

I ordered a glass of Quincy and he reached behind him for the opened bottle, pulled the cork in a manner I had never seen before — using the knuckles of his first two fingers like pliers — and slopped a measure into my glass.

I took it away to a table and sat down. I sniffed the wine and it smelled corked, that telltale rotting odour of damp basements and old rubber. Next to brimstone it is the most depressing smell on earth, especially when detected in old magnums and larger format bottles.

I returned to the counter and in my best French I said, "*Excusez-moi, mais ce vin sent le bouchon.*"

The proprietor's eyes narrow and he leans across the counter as if seeing me for the first time.

Impossible, he tells me.

Smell it for yourself, says I.

He will have nothing to do with the glass that I am sliding across the counter to him. Instead, he reaches behind to the bottle from which he had poured and sniffs that.

It's fine, he says, that's the way it's meant to smell.

Not like that, I reply. Quincy doesn't smell like that.

He shrugs.

By this time there is a communal stirring among the other patrons of the wine bar who, up to this point, have been sitting quietly smoking their Gauloises and reading their newspapers. They must have sensed an imminent exchange of philosophical views. The French love an argument. A couple move towards the counter to satisfy their curiosity.

Now that he has an audience the proprietor suddenly takes an interest in my glass. He picks it up, sniffs it and puts it down again.

It's fine, he says.

By this time I'm beginning to feel hot under the collar but I am determined to stand my ground.

The proprietor looks at the couple who are eyeing me and the offending glass. His glance invests them as allies. He shrugs an eloquent Gallic shrug that speaks volumes: Anglo-Saxons, says the lift of the shoulders and the raising of the eyes to the ceiling, what do they know about wine? They are questioning our judgement: we, who have taken in wine with our mother's milk, whose grandfathers and great-grandfathers and their fathers before them, going back to Charlemagne and Pepin III, have grown grapes gloriously from Champagne to Cahors, from the Coteaux d'Ancenis to the Côte de Provence, our forebears who pruned the vines with their teeth and pressed the juice with their feet, feet that marched with Napoleon triumphantly through Europe....

Obviously, the silent invocation of his ancestors causes some ancient anger at the memory of Agincourt to boil up within him, because he turns his back on me and begins to gesticulate through the serving hatch.

He wheels around suddenly, picks up the glass and sniffs it again, then hands it to the couple, demanding that they corroborate his statement that this is what Quincy should smell and taste like. They take the glass and sniff tentatively at it. They hand it on to other people in the bar who are now eager to have their say. Soon the glass is going from hand to hand and everyone is smelling it and passing comment.

I am standing in the centre of this maelstrom of oenological debate, the blood pulsing in my cheeks. As the noise mounts I back towards the door. But before I leave I get in my parting shot.

"I come from Canada. And we know what bad wine is!"

> "I come from Canada. And we know what bad wine is!"

This experience did not deter me from sending wine back in a three-star Paris restaurant. I was part of a group of Commonwealth Holiday Inn executives who had been invited to Lucas-Carton — in the Place Madeleine. Our host, who supplied the hotel chain with wine, ordered a Château Léoville-Poyferré 1971. Two bottles were required to serve us all. I can't recall if the second bottle was tasted or not, but when my glass was filled I smelled cork. Since the host was at the far end of the table, I made eye contact with a waiter and suggested that we needed another bottle. At first he thought I was ordering a third bottle, but when he learned that I was querying the health of the wine his demeanour changed. Frostily, he lifted my glass from the table and removed it. I saw him take it to a work station and have a hurried consultation with the maître d'. They looked in my direction and then the maître d' took a sniff of the glass. I could see from his expression that he too found the wine to be corked. The glasses that had been poured from the tainted bottle were whisked away and a fresh bottle brought.

Moral: Even the best restaurants in the world can serve a bad bottle.

The only wine that has made the earth move for me was a Sauvignon Blanc.

It was in Chile, a country I visited for the first time in March 1985. I had toured several of the wineries that were just beginning to make an impact on the international export market,

Concha Y Toro, Vina San Pedro, Santa Rita, Valdivieso, Tarapacá, Undurraga, Canepa.

At that time the Torres winery in Curicó, a two-hour drive south of Santiago, was the Mecca for all Chilean winemakers. The house of Torres, headquartered in Vilfranca del Penedes near Barcelona, was the first European winery to buy vineyard land and set up a winery operation in Chile. In 1978 they purchased a 100-hectare property that used to be Vina Maquehua. Miguel A. Torres began replanting the vineyards a year later and, equally important, he brought in state-of-the-art wine making equipment from Europe — stainless steel tanks and fermenters, Vaslin horizontal presses, refrigeration plants and American oak barriques for ageing the reds — equipment that would revolutionize the entire Chilean wine industry.

In the late 1970s Chilean wines still spent an inordinate time resting in large oak vats made of *rauli*, a native hardwood beech, usually of venerable age, or in concrete tanks in varying states of disrepair. The white wines all had a maderized taste — a sherry-like flavour — from long exposure to air, and the reds were plummy and tired. Like the Greeks with retsina, Chileans' palates had become accustomed to the flavours their local wine industry produced and they prized them; but the international market was looking for fresh, fruity wines. Torres showed the Chileans how to make them.

Jan Read, in his book *Chilean Wines*, wrote:

The entry of Torres into the Chilean wine industry was much more than the arrival on the scene of a foreign firm. Miguel A. Torres is one of the world's most accomplished winemakers and for the first time in Chile he set about making white wines by "cold fermentation," so exploiting the remarkable quality of the fruit to the full. The new white wines were immediately successful in foreign markets, and other enlightened Chilean wine firms were quick to consult with him and to follow his example. What has recently set the seal on his achievement has been the award, in competition with wines from all over the world, of no less than one gold and two silver medals for Torres red, white and rosé wines from Chile at the 1985 Olympia Wine Fair in London, together with a special award for "exceptional wine-making."

So I was looking forward to tasting these wines. As luck would have it, Miguel A. Torres was at the winery for the crush and he invited me to a tasting at the house of his vineyard manager on a Sunday evening. It was a modest two-storey building set by the vineyard.

The first wine he poured was a 1993 Sauvignon Blanc that had spent four months in oak barrels.

Miguel Torres is an intense and very serious man with a warm and ready smile. He looks like a young Pierre Elliott Trudeau and has the same charisma. As we sipped the wine and Miguel spoke about his plans to expand the vineyard, I suddenly heard a rumbling noise outside, like the sound of an express train approaching from a distance. I could feel the floor trembling under my feet and the wine in the glass began to agitate.

"What's that?" I asked.

"Oh, that's an earthquake," said Miguel.

He kept talking and the noise got louder. The framed pictures on the wall started bouncing and glasses began to slide off the shelves.

"Don't you think we should get out of here?" I asked.

"It's nothing," said Miguel. "It will pass. I've been through worse than this in Japan."

The whole room began to shake and the light sconces burst from the plaster. Instinctively, we both put our hands over our glasses as dust began to fall from the ceiling.

"I think it's time we went outside," said Miguel, when the noise became deafening.

I shall never forget the feeling of that earthquake under my feet. A winemaker in California once described watching the movement of a quake through his hillside vineyard. The vines rose like a wave and settled back, "like the shudder along a horse's flank." The experience for me was more like standing on a water bed. My feet seemed to sink into the ground as it swelled and heaved under me. The solid earth seemed to have turned molten. I looked at the road and the tarmac had separated from the ground and was waving a foot above it like a black ribbon in the wind. I had the terrifying vision of the earth opening up, of my dropping into the crevasse and then it closing over me.

The solid earth seemed to have turned molten.

We later learned that the quake was Force 8 on the Richter scale and had lasted for two minutes. The epicentre occurred at sea, off the coast of Valparaiso. It had been particularly violent, since the movement of the plates was simultaneously lateral and vertical. That evening Chilean wineries lost millions of litres of wine as tanks twisted and collapsed and barrels were split asunder by the force of the earth's movement.

The wine in our glass, ironically, was called "Bellaterra."

In the aftermath of the earthquake, Chile's president, General Pinochet, declared a midnight curfew to discourage looting. Anyone found on the streets after that time would be shot. I made a point of getting back to the Sheraton Hotel in Santiago in time. That night the city went through the aftershocks. When I awoke next morning my bed was on the other side of the room and every dresser drawer had slid open. The Swedish Davis Cup team, Max Wielander and his team mates, had been staying at the hotel and had taken the first flight home, forfeiting their match against the local Chileans.

It was in the bar of the Hotel Sheraton that I had my first Pisco Sour, a refreshing aperitif that has no equal in hot climates. Pisco is the local brandy made in the north of Chile (also in Peru and Bolivia), mainly from the Moscatel grape. It has the Muscat bouquet and a flavour of perfumed plum and bitter almond. Mixed with lime juice and served iced cold it tastes great.

Here's a simple recipe for Pisco Sour: one third Pisco, two-thirds freshly squeezed lime juice over ice. Shaken, not stirred (which was the reaction I had after seeing David Cronenberg's movie *Crash*).

Sauternes

> "Time spent without a glass of wine is time wasted."
> ALBERT EINSTEIN

Sweet wines are the alpha and omega of the wine lover's experience. I would like to bet that the first wine you ever enjoyed was sweet. As our taste becomes more sophisticated our palates dry out; but as still more years go by we begin to appreciate sweet wines again. Not the syrupy stuff we enjoyed in our entry-level years but the great dessert wines of the world — Sauternes, Late Harvest Riesling, Tokaji, Icewine, Liqueur Muscat. To use a musical analogy, we are introduced to classical music by the tuneful confections of Tchaikovsky. Then we graduate to Beethoven, Mozart and Brahms. As our musical tastes become more eclectic we begin to listen to Mahler and Wagner, and then to the moderns; but as we age we return to rediscover Tchaikovsky.

The greatest of all sweet wines is Château d'Yquem, the only wine in the Bordeaux classification of 1855 to be elevated to the status of a Premier Grand Cru — above the four Grands Crus of

the Médoc and Graves. That great
American oenophile-President,
Thomas Jefferson, had already
recognised Yquem as the best
wine of the Sauternes region
sixty-eight years before the official classification. He also predicted the rankings for red
Bordeaux, according to James M.

> **The greatest of all sweet wines is Château d'Yquem.**

Gabler in his study, *Passions — The Wines and Travels of Thomas Jefferson*: "He categorized only four vineyards of first quality: Château Margaux [Margau], Latour [La Tour de Ségur], Lafite [La Fite] and Haut-Brion [Hautbrion]." Jefferson planted vineyards at Monticello, Gabler tells us, "and experimented with grape grow-ing in his Paris garden on the Champs Elysées with vine cuttings from such famous vineyards as Montrachet, Chambertin, Clos de Vougeot, Hochheim and Rudesheim" — among his favourite wines. Can you imagine Bill Clinton pottering around a vineyard in the White House garden or making a pronouncement such as this: "No nation is drunken where wine is cheap; and none sober, where the dearness of wine substitutes ardent spirits as the com-mon beverage."

Jefferson acted as the Robert Parker of his day to Presidents Washington, Adams, Madison and Monroe, buying wines for the White house cellar directly from the producers. He also bought for himself. In 1787, a year when Yquem produced 150,000 bot-tles (today the Château averages 75,000 bottles) he purchased 250 bottles. Two years later he was buying 360 bottles for the President and 120 for himself. During his eight years as President of the United States, Jefferson bought 20,000 bottles of wine from Europe's best vineyards.

Thomas Jefferson, where are you now that we really need you?

As with all breakthroughs in beverage technology, the discovery of sweet wines was either made by the Church or it was accidental. Usually because some monk or bishop forgot to do something. At Schloss Johannisberg in the Rheingau stands an equestrian statue to an anonymous harvest messenger who arrived too late in the 1760s to proclaim the picking date. The Prince-Abbot of Fulda, who gave permission for the harvest to begin, was somewhat dilatory and when he finally dispatched his messenger after frantic requests from monasteries up and down the Rhine the poor man was kidnapped on the highway by bandits. He was held for two weeks. When he was finally released, the grapes were rotting in the vineyards (with botrytis). But the frugal monks went ahead and made wine from them anyway. And the wine they produced from these desiccated clusters was the best they had ever tasted. Thus the concept of Auslese, Beerenauslese and Trockenbeerenauslese was born!

Then there is the the legend of Tokaji which sounds as if it could be the script for a Mel Brooks movie: Around 1650 the ruler of Transylvania, Prince Rákócozi, postponed the harvest at his Tokaji estate of Oremus to the end of November because of the threat of enemy attacks from the Turks. Another version talks of a ruler whose name was Zssuzsanna Lorantfly, a priest who doubled as the estate winemaker, who made the decision to delay the harvest.

James Gabler relates a story along the same lines about the serendipitous discovery of noble rot in the vineyards of Château d'Yquem. The owner of the property, the Marquis de Lur-Saluces, was delayed on his return from a trip to Russia in 1847 and his workers were waiting impatiently for his order to begin the harvest. The grapes were over-ripe and had been attacked by a strange fungus. Notwithstanding their sorry condition, the Marquis ordered the harvest to take place and the wine made. What was produced was amazing in its concentration and flavour, creating the reputation of Château d'Yquem for all time.

...all wine lovers have to taste Yquem once in their life.

Just as all men have to own a sports car once in their lives and all women have to go blond, all wine lovers have to taste Yquem once in their life. Once tasted, never forgotten.

When the 1967 Château d'Yquem was put on general release in 1972 in Liquor Control Board of Ontario stores, it was priced at $17.85 a bottle. The 1967 Château Mouton-Rothschild in the same catalogue was going for $15.20 a bottle and the same vintage of Château Haut-Brion and Margaux for $14.60. Today the 1967 d'Yquem would cost $1,200 a bottle if you could find it, and I wouldn't even think of pulling the cork on a 1967 First Growth claret for fear of what it might taste like.

I remember picking up a bottle of the '67 Yquem in 1980 as a "thank you" gift for a fishing weekend my friend Gordon Pape had invited me on. It cost me $50 at the Vintages store next to the *Toronto Star* building. As a financial guru and investment advisor, Gordon knows the current value of that bottle. It's still in his cellar. I am waiting for an invitation to drink it with him.

There is no question that certain wines, like classic cars, do appreciate if they are made to last the long haul. But wines today are not made to last, not as they were before 1975. That was the watershed year in Bordeaux when virtually everybody began to destem their grapes to cut down the amount of tannin in the wine. Tannin gives red wine its longevity. When you see very old reds with sediment in the bottle, this is tannin and colouring matter that has precipitated out over the years. It will taste bitter apart from muddying the wine if it's stirred up. (Next time you decant to separate the wine from the sediment pour the sludge that is left in the bottom of the bottle and taste it. Apart from feeling muddy in the mouth it will be very bitter.)

Those wicker baskets much beloved by the more pretentious

restaurants were invented as a means of carrying wine to table in the same position that the bottle had rested in the cellar. The butler would gently slide the wine from its bin and place it in the cradle so as not to disturb the sediment. He would carry the wine to the dining room and remove the lead capsule and the cork while the bottle rested in the prone position. By carefully pouring he could avoid any sediment streaming into the glass.

Nowadays wine cradles are virtually useless since most restaurants don't keep their wines long enough to throw a sediment. Those wicker contraptions merely take up space on the table.

But to get back to Yquem. Few wine lovers would contest the statement that Château d'Yquem makes the world's finest sweet wine. "Noble" is an adjective that springs to mind, as in "noble rot" (*pourriture noble*), the beneficent mould that grows on the skins of grapes. This fungus-like growth, *botrytis cinerea*, occurs in damp, humid conditions with sunny afternoons. The spores of the fungus puncture the skin of the berries allowing the water to evaporate, thus concentrating the sugars and acids. Conditions in Sauternes and Barsac and certain parts of the Rhine and Moselle, Austria's Burgenland and Hungary's Tokaji are highly conducive to the occurrence of botrytis. (In California they have tried to replicate this wonder of Nature by spraying bunches of harvested grapes with tomato juice, with varying degrees of success.)

Haunting the Christie's auctions in London I had heard about the legendary Yquem of the 1921 vintage.

In *Sauternes, A study of the great sweet wines of Bordeaux*, Jeffrey Benson and Alastair Mackenzie wrote, "1921: One of the greatest vintages. Picking started 15 September. An exceptionally hot summer." Michael Broadbent has written about this wine, "Surely the greatest?"

I was to try it in the most unusual of places. A friend of mine in London, Martin Stansfeld, invited me to his family home in Scotland for Christmas in the mid-1960s. The family lived on an estate not far from Aberdeen with its own salmon stream running through it.

The first day there Martin and I put on wellington boots, grabbed a couple of rods and went down to the weir to try our luck. Although there was no snow, the weather was frigid. Trying to find a suitable spot for casting, I fell into the weir.

I have never been so cold in my life, and it took a couple of tots of malt whisky to get the circulation going once I got back to the house and out of the wet clothes.

Needless to say, the incident became a major topic of conversation at the dinner table as any minor deviation from the norm seems to be at such gatherings. My host's father, a very gracious man who enjoyed playing dictionary games, was intrigued by the incident and made me recount it in great detail that night, much to my mounting embarrassment.

"I have something in the cellar that might amuse you."

Perhaps he recognized my discomfiture because he said to me, "I hear from Martin that you like wine. I have something in the cellar that might amuse you."

He returned with a bottle of Château d'Yquem 1921.

I had heard that there were magnificent cellars in Scotland but I was not prepared for this.

The wine sparkled like an amethyst in the bottle. It was unlike anything I have ever tasted. I can still conjure to memory the first sensation. The nose reminded me of the caramelized sugar on top of crême brulé with a suggestion of dried apricots and honey. It was ravishingly sweet, not in a cloying way, but beautifully balanced, mouth-filling with cleansing acidity that drew out the end taste for an astonishing length of time.

I remember everybody at the table staring at the logs burning in the grate, sipping the wine in silent reverence.

Another house guest that Christmas was Dr. Edward De Bono who told me about a new philosophy he was propounding. He called it "lateral thinking," a mode of thinking which he had developed as a new approach to problem solving; and he spent a lot of time explaining to me what he meant. We used to go for long walks on the moors and he would give me examples to illustrate this new way of reasoning. He told me that our usual mode of thought is deductive, vertical, proceeding in a straight line. There are certain problems that cannot be solved by this method. You have to break out of the formulaic approach that is based on rational modes of thought and has no room for imagination or creative leaps of insight. At the table he posed a problem: he gave me a piece of paper with a slot cut out measuring four inches by one-quarter of an inch. He then gave me an unpeeled banana and a knife. "Now," he said, "I want you to feed the banana through the slot in the simplest way you can."

Given what I had to work with my inclination was to slice the banana lengthwise in narrow enough strips to enable them to slide through the slot in the paper.

When I proposed this solution Edward said, "You don't need to cut the banana."

There was no way that I could see how you could get the whole banana through the slot. Then Edward showed me. He placed the knife at one end of the paper to weigh it down. Grasping the opposite edge of the paper he pushed it towards the anchored end. As the paper bent the slot curled open, becoming large enough for his free hand to push the banana through.

My first impulse was to cry, "Foul!" I didn't realize I was allowed to bend the paper. And when you're given a knife, your natural response is that it is a tool for cutting. But I was thinking vertically; I had defined the paper as a two-dimensional shape. By thinking laterally, Edward had broken out of the preconceived definitions and made it into a three-dimensional form. The knife worked well as a weight to immobilize the paper so that it could be bent with one hand.

I have thought a lot about what Edward De Bono told me that

night and I have tried to switch into lateral mode whenever I come up against a problem I can't solve by conventional means.

I once saw these principles applied to solving a highly unusual problem. A landscape gardener had an aerial photograph of the Buckingham Palace grounds. He wanted to find out the amount of space an ornamental lake took up in the garden, but he could not get access to the grounds to make the measurements himself. He knew the total area of the garden because that was a matter of public record, but the lake was not a uniform shape.

He studied the photo and thought hard how he could relate the known overall surface area to that of the unknown, irregularly shaped body of water.

And then it hit him.

He needed a jeweller's scale and a pair of sharp scissors.

He cut out the total area of the garden and weighed it on the scale. Then he took the photo and carefully cut around the lake and weighed that piece. From the two weights he now had the ratio of the total garden area to the water surface. It was then a simple mathematical calculation to determine the area of the ornamental lake.

When I first arrived in Toronto in 1976 you had to fill out a form to buy a bottle of wine. The Liquor Control Board of Ontario stores were the dreariest, most uninviting places imaginable. No bottles were visible; nothing to suggest that you were in a wine store. You had to consult what looked like a railway time table for a list of available products, write down the wine and the product number, your name and address. Then you had to take your docket

Liquor Control Board stores were the dreariest, most uninviting places imaginable.

to the counter where you presented it to some surly fellow who looked as if he'd rather be bowling. He would disappear into the back and emerge with a brown paper bag. He would slip it down surreptitiously to give you a quick look at the label and then cover it again, for all the world as if he were selling you a girlie magazine.

The only bright spot twenty years ago was the Rare Wine & Spirits store in a basement next to The Old Fish Market on Market Street. At least you could see the bottles even though they were locked away in glass display cases like valuable museum pieces.

You could not buy the wines by the case there, I recall; three bottles was the limit. Whether this was another form of government control or a democratic gesture to ensure that everybody had the chance to buy the meagre amount the LCBO imported I never knew.

Today the Liquor Control Board of Ontario prides itself on being the largest single purchaser of beverage alcohol in the world. They operate 595 stores around the province and employ some 4,500 people. The Board is a $2 billion business which in this financial year expects to pass on to the Ontario Treasury $700 million in the taxes it collects on beverage alcohol, close to 2 per cent of the provincial budget.

The LCBO is in a uniquely uncomfortable position. As a government enterprise it is a wholesaler, distributor and retailer of beverage alcohol. Yet it is at the same time a regulator and monitor. The government sets the hours when wine, beer and spirits can be sold and the LCBO chooses the products it believes consumers want.

While the rest of Canada is lurching slowly towards a free market in wine (Alberta first), Ontario dithers and will probably be the last of the provinces to privatize. Personally, I would like to see a mixed system, with the Liquor Board taking care of the mass market imported wines and Ontario wines, ensuring that they are available in stores throughout Ontario. Importing agents should have the right to set up their own storefront operations and sell directly to the public. The same for the trade commissions in Toronto and Ottawa. Wines should be available in "off-licence" premises in restaurants, hotels and fine food stores.

But I can't see this happening in my lifetime — not in Ontario.

Beer

> "I have nothing to offer you but blood, sweat and beers."
> WINSTON CHURCHILL

The evolution of the wine drinker is based on sex.

As a student you drink beer. Beer is a ritualistic beverage, consumed by men in groups. Wine is a form of courtship. A man will order wine in a restaurant when he takes a woman to dinner. We come to wine through beer and certainly, thinking back to my own undergraduate days in Montreal, wine was not the beverage of choice, except when you were dating and wished to make a good impression. By ordering wine you hoped you would appear sophisticated, a man of the world — provided you could navigate your way through the wine list without embarrassment. But then in those days you probably knew more about wine than the waiter who was serving you.

At McGill University in the late 1950s beer, not wine, was central to the success of any fraternity party. My fraternity was Zeta

Beta Tau whose house was located on Peel Street. When we were not partying there, we would drink at the old Berkeley Hotel on Sherbrooke Street or more likely at Café André, known affectionately as "The Shrine," which was within easy walking distance of the campus, around the corner from the Student Union.

The Shrine, a dark, smoky bar, was nicknamed by some inspired student after St. Joseph's Oratory — the vast cathedral that dominates the west side of Montreal's mountain overlooking Queen Mary Road. The original shrine was built in memory of Brother André, who performed many miraculous cures there. Supplicants still climb the stone steps leading up to the huge edifice on their knees. Acolytes of The Shrine frequented by McGill students were more likely to *leave* those premises on their knees.

We used to drink beer with some of our English Department professors at The Shrine, notably Harry Ritchie, who taught drama, and the poet Louis Dudek, who would read from his own works in the dim light, continuing the lecture we had just left. In those days at McGill we were more interested in poetry than politics. It was the era of Leonard Cohen and "My Fur Lady." In fact, Leonard was my fraternity brother in 1956 when I entered McGill. He had already published *Let Us Compare Mythologies* and was known as the campus Lothario, a role he has played magnificently throughout his career as a latter-day troubadour. His biographer, Ira B. Nadel, tells the story of how Leonard once approached a beautiful woman with long black hair at a cocktail party. He gently took a handful of her hair, dipped it into his wine glass and sucked the ends dry. He then walked on without a word.

Leonard could get away with that sort of thing. The Byronic gesture. When I read about this incident, it reminded me of what used to go on with the showgirls at the Folies Bergères in Paris at the turn of the century: monocled stage-door Johnnies drinking champagne out of the shoes of showgirls. It was said that the practice was initiated in England by Edward VII when he was Prince of Wales. This bizarre custom was revived during the

Flapper era. The idea is meant to be both romantic and erotic; but I have always thought of it as mildly disgusting and a terrible thing to do to champagne. It is the craven subterfuge of the foot fetishist disguised as exhibitionism, and the unfortunate lady who receives such attentions is doomed to squelch around the rest of the evening in a sodden shoe.

I can't imagine anything like this going on in Dublin, where they are very particular about their drink if not their feet. I had chosen Dublin as the place where I wanted to do post-graduate work. It was either Dublin or the Yale Drama School. Looking back on it, my decision to choose Dublin probably set me on a life course that would end, inevitably, in my becoming a wine writer. It is not a job you aspire to as soon as you leave university. It is an accidental occupation, something that you fall into, deflected from your perceived goal by an accident in life that sends you off at a tangent. Perhaps today there are schools of journalism where you can actually learn how to write about wine but for me and, I imagine, many of my colleagues for whom it is a full-time occupation and their main source of income, wine writing was not the goal of our education, our nine-to-five preoccupation.

It is an accidental occupation, something that you fall into...

In fact, wine becomes the preoccupation of every waking hour for the wine writer. It is an all-encompassing subject that seems to come up spontaneously whenever people sit down at table or hold a glass at a party. As soon as you identify yourself as a wine writer you become the target of other people's anecdotes and questions. (Invariably, "What's a good white and red under $10 these days?")

The wine writer has to make a conscious effort not to let the subject take over his or her life.

After graduating from McGill in English and Philosophy (a course of study that equips you for no trade or profession other than teaching or wine writing) I signed up for the M.Litt programme at Trinity College, Dublin. This venerable seat of learning was the Alma Mater of Jonathan Swift who, according to *The Oxford Companion of English Literature*, "was censured for offences against discipline, obtaining his degree only by special grace." Trinity's other claim to fame is that it is the repository of Ireland's most illustrious artefact, The Book of Kells, known to the students as Kelly's Book. The movie *Educating Rita*, incidentally, was filmed on that campus about twenty years after I left it — without a degree, unblessed as I was by "special grace."

My thesis was to be "The Irish Influence in the plays of Eugene O'Neill." To put myself in the right frame of mind for scholarship I had spent my graduation summer at Harvard taking a course in Greek tragedy. The Greek professor who gave the course set me a term paper entitled, "The Anagnorisis in Ezra Pound's translation of Sophocles' *The Women of Trachis*." I had to look up *anagnorisis* in a dictionary; it means revelation or dénouement. I recall that Shelley had a copy of Sophocles in his pocket when he was drowned while sailing near Spezzia. Now I understand why.

Dublin in 1959 was a city of pubs and theatres and easy conversation, far removed from the sectarian violence that was to come. The relationship of Dublin to the students from overseas (England as well as North America and African countries — I had a good friend who was a PhD student from Egypt) was well captured by J. P. Donleavy in his riotous first novel, *The Ginger Man*. Donleavy left Dublin the summer before I arrived. I was to meet him years later at the CBC in Toronto when he was on a book tour and we reminisced about those Dublin years. He told me that it was Brendan Behan who was instrumental in getting *The Ginger Man* published. He had broken into the cottage in the Wicklow Hills that Donleavy was renting, looking for something to drink, and discovered the manuscript. Donleavy found him asleep with the pages strewn around him.

The flat that Donleavy lived in and described in *The Ginger Man* was rented in my time by a Pakistani student who shared it with a Nigerian. The three of us once visited "The Four Provinces," a rather seedy dance hall on the north side of the city, and picked up three sisters whom we brought back to the flat. They were so appalled by the state of the place that they insisted on cleaning it up before we partied.

Trinity College was the Protestant university and University College Dublin was the Catholic institution; there was little contact between the two student bodies. We drank in different pubs and held our parties in different places. Now the two universities have amalgamated.

At Trinity, I was allocated a tutor whose specialty was eighteenth century English literature. He had little sympathy for living writers and none at all if they were American. His name was Pyle and I don't think he liked me. Actually, I don't think he liked students in general. I had to inform him that Eugene O'Neill had died six years earlier.

The first assignment Pyle set me was to read through all the extant Greek tragedies. There are seventy-two plays by Aeschylus that are known, but mercifully for me only seven have survived. Euripides is said to have written ninety, but we know only eighteen. Seven plays by Sophocles remain. For the first six months of my stay in Dublin I dutifully went to the library and ploughed through the Greeks and then the Irish playwrights, John Millington Synge (a TCD man), William Butler Yeats and Sean O'Casey.

Dublin in those days was a very sociable city. You could meet and talk to anyone in the pubs, unlike in London. I was introduced to Noel Coward in a pub called "The Bailey" when he was in town for the opening of one of his plays. The Bailey was, and still is, one of Dublin's more famous watering holes. It stands opposite Davy Byrne's, immortalized in James Joyce's *Ullyses*, but it is The Bailey that is home to a Joycean treasure — the door to Leopold Bloom's house, saved from the wrecker's ball. It was in The Bailey that I would meet Brendan Behan who would play a significant role in my life as an aspiring impresario on my return to Canada in the fall of 1960.

Hilary Frayne (now Ontario's Lieutenant-Governor, Hilary Weston) was a Dublin model then and I used to watch her sashaying down the cat-walk, since I was going out with one of her colleagues, a beautiful young woman named Adrienne Ring. My mode of transportation at that time was a motor bike. Actually, it wasn't so much a motor bike as a motorized bicycle, an NSU Quickly which had a top speed of 32 miles an hour — downhill with the wind behind it. But it got me around. There was a pillion on the back which was not meant for passengers but Adrienne could sit sidesaddle and tuck her legs up for the short trip from my house to hers.

It was the bike that was my undoing as a scholar. I used to carry my work back from the library to my room wedged under the pillion. It had a metal spring that held down books and manuscripts, rather like the business end of a mousetrap. One day after a vigorous discussion over Guinness I was driving back to my new digs in Hatch Lane, behind the UCD dormitories. The road was bumpy and there was a high wind — indeed, a blustering gale. I was so intent on avoiding oncoming traffic and staying upright that I failed to see that my thesis was blowing away page by page from the back of the bike.

... my thesis was blowing away page by page...

When I got home there was nothing left. And I had no copy. In those days before computers you pecked out the words laboriously on a typewriter. Maybe it was a Freudian act, leaving the manuscript in such a precarious place. I was not cut out to be an academic. With my thesis gone and without the will to start again, I gave myself up to the city of Dublin. Which meant the life of the pub.

I soon acquired a liking for Guinness which in Dublin tastes different than it does in any other part of the world. They say it's the water from the River Liffey; but there is no comparison in flavour to what they make at the Park Royal brewery in London. You can carve your initials in the creamy head of a Dublin pint, down the whole thing and they'll still be there in the bottom of the glass.

In those days they had inspectors who would go around to ensure that the publicans were serving Guinness at the right temperature (65°, about the same temperature that is best for red Bordeaux or Burgundy).

My first rooming house in Dublin was in Ballsbridge, not far from the show grounds where they held the annual Dog Show. This event in the Spring was extremely well attended because until 1961 it was the only place in Ireland where you could get a drink legally on St Patrick's Day. Men who had never patted a dog in their lives thirsted to get into the show grounds for that event.

There is a story that Brendan Behan was at the show one year and accidentally stepped on a prize poodle. He turned around and shouted, "Who the fuck brought the fuckin' dog?"

In those days Dublin pubs had to close between 2:30 and 3:30 p.m. This was called Holy Hour. But the publicans had solved the problem in true Dublin fashion: rather than locking their clientele out, they locked them in.

The other strange anomaly about Dublin drinking hours was the *bona fide* system. Until 1960 the pubs closed at 11 p.m. If you were a bona fide traveller you could drink until midnight in establishments that were located at least three miles outside the city limits. Which meant that when the city pubs closed at 11 p.m. there was a mad dash to the pubs in the outlying areas to spend another forty-five minutes carousing. The most famous destination for Dublin's dedicated drinkers was The Silver Tassey at Foxrock, eight miles from St. Stephen's Green. You approached it on Ireland's first dual carriageway en route for Bray.

Needless to say, the slaughter on the roads caused by this nightly exodus by drivers in various stages of intoxication was enormous and had to be stopped. The government in its wisdom extended Dublin's drinking hours to 11:30 to make the trip to the bona fides unnecessary.

The passing of this old institution was marked by huge parties at the bona fides ringing the city. I was taken to one such pub on the last night of the bona fides by Garech Browne, a member of the Guinness family. I never saw Garech drink Guinness; his preference was for Power Irish whiskey. The pub he had chosen was stocked with Power, hundreds of bottles displayed on the shelves around the walls, gleaming like amber necklaces. The place was mobbed. By the early hours of the morning there was nothing left.

I had met Garech Browne through my friend Adrienne and when I decided that the halls of academe no longer beckoned me I spent much time in his company. As a Guinness heir he had no need to work.

Garech was an Irish nationalist, a cultural nationalist, that is. He would scour the country in his black Mercedes looking for Aeolian pipe music and the musicians who played it, determined to preserve the traditional music. He wore an Aran sweater and Donegal tweed trousers most of the time, held up by a *crios*, a woven length of patterned wool that you tied twice around your waist as a belt. He had a thatch of unruly blond hair and an infectious, explosive laugh. Whenever I tried to imitate the Irish brogue he would double over with laughter and call me an "eejit." I think that Garech was my age (21) but there was a Peter Pan quality about him, or maybe an overgrown leprechaun, and he could have been much older.

Every year Garech held a harvest party for the workers on his estate to which he invited the musician friends he had collected on his nightly rounds of the ceilidh clubs. He insisted that everyone come dressed in national costume. The only national costume exotic enough to wear to the event that I could lay claim to was Russian; so I went to a theatrical costumier and hired a Cossack outfit, complete with red leather boots, lambswool hat and saber. (In retrospect, this was akin to my dressing up as a Nazi SS officer, since my Russian grandparents had been subjected to the pogroms in the early years of this century.)

Adrienne accompanied me to the party dressed as an Irish colleen. We danced and drank and had a whale of a time. There were fiddlers and Uileann pipers and step dancers and lots of food and endless supplies of Guinness and Irish whiskey. When it came time to leave, we were offered a lift home by an ageing American piper who had flown over specially for the event.

Garech's estate was high in the Wicklow Hills and the roads were narrow and winding. The American piper, tired from his exertions by four o'clock in the morning, to say nothing of the whiskey he had consumed, drove into a ditch and immediately fell asleep over the steering wheel. There was no way we could open the driver's door to remove him so that Adrienne could drive (I did not have a licence). We got out of the car and waited to flag down a passing vehicle.

There I stood in the mists of early morning, dressed in my Cossack outfit complete with saber, in the middle of nowhere trying to thumb a lift. The occasional car that passed took one look at this crazed apparition and sped off into the night, invoking the name of St. Christopher to protect them against goblins and little people. One car did slow down. The driver wound down his window and peered out at me. His wife sat next to him, clutching her purse to her chest, staring straight ahead.

"Jasus, would you look at that," I heard him say, before he roared off up the hill.

The morning air was cold and fog was rising from the damp ground. Adrienne was shivering. We checked on the American piper who was still sleeping peacefully, snoring into the steering wheel. We covered him with a travelling rug and began to walk towards Dublin.

Suddenly we saw headlights coming up towards us.

"You'd better stand behind me," said Adrienne.

She waved the car down and it stopped. It was the local Gardai. Two policeman with large red faces. They looked as if they had been celebrating too. Their caps were on the back seat, their ties were pulled down and the top button of their shirts undone.

They got out of the car unsteadily and took out their notebooks.

"And what do we have here?"

The cadence was unmistakably Cork.

They were weaving about, thumbing through their notebooks as Adrienne tried to explain our predicament without incriminating the American piper.

"And yer man," said the other, pointing at me with his pencil. "Does he understand English?"

"I'm in national costume," I said, mustering as much dignity as I could under the circumstances.

"And what nation would that be, sir?"

"Russian."

They began to laugh.

"Do you dance?"

"Dance?"

"With yer red boots, do you dance?"

I was beginning to get angry. The effects of the party were wearing off. I could see the gooseflesh on Adrienne's arms and I was getting cold too. Then a thought occurred to me.

"Are you really policemen? How do we know you're not in

fancy dress like us?"

"Because we've got identification," said one.

"May I see it?"

They began reaching for their wallets and then started patting their pockets. They had forgotten to bring their identification.

"We are gardai certainly, sir. You see, here's me notebook. We have a radio in the car."

"What would your superiors think if you went on duty without your cards?"

I was milking the situation for all it was worth. They fidgeted like Laurel and Hardy caught in the act.

"We won't say a word if you give us a lift back to Dublin," said Adrienne.

"It will be our pleasure, miss."

*B*ut for a pint of Guinness I could have competed for Ireland in the 1960 Rome Olympics — on the fencing team. My father was born in Belfast before Partition and although I held a British passport in 1960, legally I could have had an Irish one which would have made me eligible to represent the land of the shamrock.

Ireland's Olympic team was chosen from members of the Trinity College fencing team. My weapon was the epée. I had learned to fence as a counsellor at summer camp in Brandon, Vermont, in my second year at McGill. I had no knowledge of the sport until I was thrown in at the deep end. The regular fencing counsellor was fired for unspecified misdemeanours and the owner of the camp asked if anyone knew how to fence. As a "specialist" counsellor you were paid more, so I said I could fence although I had never lifted a foil.

The head counsellor showed me how to hold the weapon, how to get into the en garde *position, how to thrust and how to parry. Voila!*

I was a fencer. As long as I could stay one step ahead of the kids.

I enjoyed the idea of fencing and when I found out that Trinity had a fencing club I joined. Our instructor made us stand in the en garde position with the tip of our blades a quarter of an inch from the wall. He would hold a piece of paper with his thumb and when he released it we had to lunge and skewer the paper to the wall. It sounds easy but you need great speed and agility to perform this exercise.

Three members of the Irish team had been chosen and it was down to the final weapon — epée. There was to be a fence-off between the captain of the team and me. We had both been at Neary's having a Guinness at lunch. Neary's served wonderful ham sandwiches, thickly cut, which were a boon for hungry students. The half pint of Guinness went down very well with it. "A bird never flew on one wing," is an old Irish expression, so I had the other half.

I lost the bout and with it the opportunity to be an Irish Olympian.

In the back bar of Jammet's, a Dublin restaurant that no longer exists, you could order oysters with soda bread and game birds like plover and teal. They were served to you at the marble-topped counter. This inner sanctum was a meeting place for writers and would-be writers. It was in Jammet's that I met Liam O'Flaherty. He was sixty-three then and the reigning lion of Irish letters.

O'Flaherty was the Irish Hemingway, a great bull of man with a florid complexion and a luxuriant growth of white hair. He had led the kind of life that looks good on the back of paperback novels. His biography reads: "O'Flaherty rejected his training for the priesthood and embarked on a varied career as a soldier in World War I and an international wanderer in South America, Canada, the United States and the Near East. He laboured in occupations such as lumberjack, hotel porter, miner, factory worker, dishwasher, bank clerk and deckhand. After taking part in a revolutionary bombing plot in Ireland, O'Flaherty settled in England in

1922...." There is some dispute about the bombing. Another version has it that O'Flaherty was expelled to England for a violent act. Leading a group of unemployed workers he seized a government building in Dublin and hoisted the red flag. Whatever the reason, he had cemented his reputation as a man of action and a committed Republican. The novel that O'Flaherty is best remembered for is *The Informer*, published in 1925. The story concerns a dim-witted Irish revolutionary who sells out his friend during "The Troubles." The book was made into a Hollywood movie ten years later and won Academy Awards for its director, John Ford, scriptwriter Dudley Nichols, Max Steiner's music and Victor McLaglen's performance as Gypo Nolan, the anti-hero of the title.

As an aspiring writer I was in awe of Liam O'Flaherty. I had been introduced to him at The Bailey. When I returned to Dublin from a trip to Israel (my parents had given me money to travel for my twenty-first birthday) I went straight to Jammet's to see who was there.

O'Flaherty was sitting on a bar stool with a woman in her forties who wore a red dress.

In Dublin there are no secrets and when I walked into the bar, O'Flaherty bellowed, "Ah, the Israeli spy returns!"

He invited me to sit down and bought me a drink. Then he suggested we all go to the Russell Hotel for dinner. I was wearing cotton pants, desert boots, an open-necked shirt and the heavy wool cardigan my sister had knitted for me when I told her I was going to Dublin to study. It had a large cowl-like collar, the kind of sweater worn by curling teams.

> ...O'Flaherty bellowed, "Ah the Israeli spy returns!"

When we got to the Russell, then Dublin's most prestigious hotel, the maître d' took one look at the way I was dressed and told O'Flaherty that I could not be allowed into the dining room.

I needed a tie.

"Send a cabriolet to my apartments and have a cravat picked up for my young friend," he shouted.

Cowed, the maître d' ushered the three of us to a table in the corner as far out of sight of other diners as it was possible to be.

We ordered steak and a bottle of red wine. I don't know why O'Flaherty had invited me along since his attentions were concentrated on the woman in the red dress, whose name was Maura. She would make involuntary starts throughout the meal as if her chair were wired for electricity. It occurred to me that she was fighting off his advances under the tablecloth.

At the end of the meal our host suggested that we repair to The Red Barn for a nightcap. We arrived there by taxi just after 11:30 p.m. to find the bar closed. Undaunted, O'Flaherty began to pound on the door. Eventually it was opened and once the proprietor saw who was standing in the street, the door was flung wide and we were invited in.

The chairs were on the tables in the bar but a space was cleared for us and whiskey was served. O'Flaherty continued to practise his blatant seduction technique on Maura who kept laughing and pulling the hem of her skirt down. Around midnight she said she had to get back to her husband.

O'Flaherty escorted her to the street and hailed a taxi. He shook his head and shrugged as the cab pulled away.

"I have a bottle of gin at home," he said. "We'll go there."

By this time I had consumed sufficient alcohol to dull the brain. I did not need to drink gin which is a taste I really don't like. But I was curious about Liam O'Flaherty's life as a writer and flattered to be in his company.

The living room of his apartment was lined with bookshelves. *The Neighbour's Wife*, *The Black Soul*, *The Informer*, *Famine*, *Insurrection* and volumes of short stories. There were various editions in a United Nations of languages. It was an amazing sight. I had never seen anything like it before. I dreamed of the day when

I would have a novel that would be published around the world.

O'Flaherty poured the gin as I gawked at his books. He handed me a glass and I sat down on the sofa. He sat next to me and began talking about going to Hollywood in 1935 to help John Ford make the movie of his novel.

Suddenly he leaned over and kissed me on the cheek.

The accumulation of alcohol had dulled my senses and I dismissed his action as a spontaneous act of affection, something perhaps the Irish did under those circumstances. I pretended I had not noticed. How naive can you get?! He must have taken my lack of response for acquiescence because I then found myself crushed by the weight of his body, his lips glued to mine.

I began to struggle and push him off me.

"You don't want to," he said.

I wiped my lips with the back of my hand. My head was spinning and I felt like throwing up.

... something perhaps the Irish did under those circumstances.

I remember saying, "I think I'm going to be sick."

He hustled me out of the apartment and flagged down a taxi. He closed the door on me without a word.

I felt awful. My head was throbbing, my stomach was heaving in nauseous spasms. I leant my head against the cold glass of the window. The cab driver asked me where I wanted to go. I couldn't remember my own address. I wanted to be in my own bed. I wanted a bath. I felt lonely and miserable. Most of all I felt betrayed, a literary groupie who had come close to being raped.

I never saw Liam O'Flaherty again, and I cannot hear his name to this day without remembering the pressure of his wet, gin-flavoured lips against mine.

I have never been able to drink gin since then.

*E*very country has its moonshine whisky but none is more potent than Poteen, which the Irish make in illicit stills in the West. Pronounced pocheen with the stress on the second syllable, the word is derived from the pot-still, an endearing diminutive of "pot." The water-white spirit can be distilled from potatoes, vegetables, fruits, grains or anything else that contains starch or sugar.

The canny poteen makers of the Western Isles used to frustrate the revenue officers by distilling on board their boats out at sea so that the winds would disperse the tell-tale smell.

There is an old Irish joke about the police who raid a farm and uncover an illegal still. The sergeant says to the farmer, "You know why we're here, don't you?"

"I do indeed," replied the farmer. "But you've come too late. We're out of stock now."

Poteen is lethal. A Dublin friend once smuggled a bottle into England, declaring it as "holy water" from Lourdes. A good thing the customs officer did not uncork the bottle and smell.

Garech Browne introduced me to poteen. I drank a measure and immediately my throat contracted. I got a roaring headache and next morning I woke up with a pounding head and a parched throat.

In an effort to slake my thirst I drank a large glass of water. This only seemed to activate the alcohol all over again and I had two hangovers for the price of one!

Brendan Behan's undoing in Montreal was Black Velvet, a mixture of champagne and Guinness — a concoction that is an insult to both drinks. (But then who would think of putting beer and tomato juice together?)

Behan ordered it in Moishe's Steak House on the Main one frigid December night in 1960; and matters went downhill from there. His wife Beatrice threw her eyes heavenward, knowing what was to come....

I had met Brendan in The Bailey, his usual haunt. I have a copy

of *The Hostage* that he signed for me,
"To Tony
from

 rendan
ehan in the
ailey."

I had won an inter-varsity drama award for a one-act play I had written, entitled *Echo of A Sigh,* about a man in prison. This must have appealed to Behan, who had spent time in British jails for his Republican activities — he was arrested in Liverpool at the age of sixteen with a suitcase full of bomb-making equipment and sent to Borstal, where he would "find himself."

In fact, his most important works, *Borstal Boy*, *The Quare Fella* and *The Hostage,* all have to do with incarceration.

Brendan Behan was generous to young writers and enjoyed lifting a pint with anyone who would join him. His Guinness was usually augmented with a shot of Irish whiskey. He was also a great swimmer who had little fear of the cold. I once witnessed him taking a dip in the Black Rock swimming baths, outdoors on a blustery September morning. We had had breakfast together at his house to discuss his visit to Montreal to appear at McGill and Comédie Canadienne. He would take the train from New York and stay for a week.

During my senior year at McGill I had been chairman of a com mittee called Scope which brought in guest lecturers. This committee had a budget of $4,000 from the Student Society to put on events. That year I booked Ogden Nash, e.e. cummings, Josh White and a Spanish guitarist. I liked the impresario business and thought that this might make an interesting career, all the more so when my friend John Garson and I were approached by the Comédie Canadienne management to see if we would back a performance of the great Welsh actor Emlyn Williams reading from Dickens. No up-front cash was required; all expenses for ticket printing and newspaper ads would come out of the profits (if there were any).

The "Evening with Emlyn Williams" was presented under the banner of the leading cultural impresario of the time, Sol Hurok. Our names did not appear on any of the posters or advertisements, thank God, because we were both going through our final exams and our parents would not have been amused if they found out that their sons had been spending inordinate amounts of time on such a risky venture. All the more if they realized that they would have to carry the can financially if the show did not attract a decent audience.

My father saw the advertisement in the *Montreal Star* and thought it would be an interesting show. He asked me if I would like to go since it was the evening after my final exam. I told him I would be too exhausted and that John and I were thinking of getting out of Montreal to unwind.

Unable to face the consequences of our actions, John and I fled to New York. The next morning John phoned the manager of the Comédie Canadienne to find out how the show went.

"It was a sell-out," he said.

We made a profit of $6,000.

That's why I thought it would be fun to be an impresario and why I arranged for Brendan Behan to come to Montreal.

In September 1960, *The Hostage* opened in New York and Behan flew over from Dublin to help with the production. My parents were visiting New York at the time and I arranged for them to meet Behan at the Algonquin Hotel where he was staying. He was on the wagon then, enjoying being lionized by the New York media, an instant celebrity in a city that knows how to take care of its celebrities.

I arrived back in Montreal in November and began immediately to make arrangements for Behan's visit and his two appearances. I contacted an Irish club to enlist their help in spreading the word about his imminent arrival and was surprised by their cool response. They were concerned about Behan's behaviour when he was drinking: his antics might embarrass them, reflecting badly on the Montreal Irish community as a whole. I assured them that Behan had not touched a drink since he had set foot in New York. Although he had not toned down his anti-authoritarian pronouncements: at one press conference he stated that St. Patrick drove the snakes out of Ireland and they all went to New York to become policemen.

Brendan Behan arrived in Montreal with his wife, Beatrice, at the beginning of December 1960. It was fearsomely cold that winter and as he stepped off the train at Windsor Station, without a coat, all he could say was, "Jasus, Mary and Joseph."

There was no welcoming committee, no journalists or TV cameras on the platform, no crowds seeking autographs. I had informed the media about his arrival but there was little interest. After the adulation of New York and Broadway he must have felt deflated to be shrugged off by Montreal. The bitterly cold weather was a metaphor in itself. Behan loved to walk the streets and talk to strangers. The wind that slices along Sherbrooke Street in winter makes conversation painful.

I had booked the Behans into a hotel at the corner of Peel and Sherbrooke. I asked him what he would like to eat for dinner. "Steak," he said, so I booked a table for four (we were joined by an Irish friend of Behan's who lived in Montreal, named Noel) at the city's most celebrated steak house, Moishe's.

"This is a city of hatreds," said Behan, as we drove north along St. Lawrence Boulevard. "I can smell them."

He was looking tired and dispirited — which turned out to be the case because, as we sat down in the restaurant, he ordered a Black Velvet. He had not touched a drink for several months and Beatrice sighed in resignation. She knew the omens. He was back on the bottle.

After dinner Behan said he wanted to go to a bar. He pronounced the word, twisting his mouth, in a parody of a New York

accent. We drove to the nearest one. He ordered a whisky, stood
up and began to sing with his eyes closed:

"Oh the pratties they are small over here,
Oh the pratties they are small over here,
Oh the pratties they are small, but we ate them skin and all,
They were better than fuck-all, over here."

The habitués of the bar had no idea who this short, fat man
with the open-necked shirt and rumpled jacket was. But they paid
attention to him; they moved closer to hear his songs. At that
instant Brendan Behan had created a little Dublin around himself
and when we left the bar to find another one a few of his listeners attached themselves to our party.

We began to zigzag down St. Lawrence Boulevard hopping
from bar to bar. Behan would sing IRA songs and buy drinks for
anyone who sat down beside him. Our party got larger and larger as more and more interested spectators joined us.

... Brendan Behan had created a little Dublin around himself ...

At around midnight Behan
expressed a desire to see my mother.
He had been quite taken with her
when he had met her in New York, in
spite of her English accent.

"I want to see Mimi," he roared at
me.

Under other circumstances I
would have suggested that he wait
until the next day, but I had been
keeping pace with him and the idea seemed just fine.

My parents rented a small two-bedroom apartment on Queen
Mary Road in those years. I had lived there during my undergraduate days at McGill and had moved back when I returned
from Dublin.

"Brendan wants to see you," I announced to my mother, whom
the telephone had woken from a deep sleep.

"Are you all right?" she asked. "You sound hoarse."

"I'm fine. There's a few people with us. Is it all right if we come?"

They were up and dressed when we arrived at the apartment — Brendan and Beatrice, the Irish friend, myself and five other people I had never met before in my life and who spoke only French.

Brendan gave my mother a great bear hug and danced her around the room.

My mother's first instinct under such conditions was to feed everybody, so she started cooking. Every electrical appliance in the apartment seemed to be in use. It was a freezing night and everyone must have had their electric heaters on because there was a sudden power failure.

"Jasus, I'm blinded," yelled Behan, as he lumbered around in the dark.

He tripped over the coffee table and passed out. My father brought out the emergency candles and by their light we saw him laid out on the carpet like a beached whale. There was no way to move him so we decided to cover him with a blanket, put a pillow under his head and let him sleep.

The party broke up at this point and Beatrice was escorted back to the hotel by Noel.

The next morning I was awakened by the sound of cupboards banging. I went into the living room and there was Behan, stark naked, going through every cupboard in the room, looking for something to drink. My father was also awakened by the noise and quickly found a robe to cover the involuntary house guest.

"Is there anything to drink?" he enquired.

"I'm afraid not, Brendan."

"Well, have you got any steak tartare?"

My mother went to the fridge and came back with a pound of hamburger meat on a plate. She cracked a raw egg on the top and presented it to him.

That morning Behan recorded an interview with a CBC freelancer in our living room. Then it was time to join Beatrice for lunch at Desjardin's fish restaurant downtown for another CBC radio interview, this time with a young woman named Katie.

Behan seemed calm as he tucked into his food. "The Yanks are a very innocent race of people..." he said, and began to reminisce about his months in New York for the benefit of the interviewer.

The event at McGill University was scheduled for that evening and I thought, barring accidents, he could go on as scheduled, in spite of his hangover. Then the owner of the restaurant, having been told by someone who the heavy-set man with the mop of unruly hair was, sent over a tray of Irish coffees to our table with his compliments.

Behan drank four of them. It did not take much to get him drunk. There was so much alcohol in his system it was like topping up a car engine. I began to see visions of impending disaster. I phoned my contact at the university and told him that Brendan might not be able to make it for the evening's performance.

By the time we left the restaurant he was singing with his eyes closed. I knew we would have to cancel. I called the university again and told them Behan would not be able to go on. But he was determined to appear, as inebriated as he was. I drove him around the city to try and take his mind off the evening's event but nothing would stop him from fulfilling his obligation. He demanded I drive him to the university and when I demurred he threatened to get out of the car while it was still moving.

... he was determined to appear, as inebriated as he was.

I drove him to McGill and I wish I hadn't. A crowd of disgruntled students was milling about the Roddick Gates. They had been informed of the last-minute cancellation and were angry and disappointed. But when they recognized Brendan Behan's face in the passenger seat of the car the cry went up, "He's here! He's here!" There was a mad stampede up the drive to the main steps and into Moyse Hall.

Behan marched into the hall as the students scrambled into the seats. He clambered up onto the stage and looked out over the audience. He was sweating visibly and was unsteady on his feet. He spoke incoherently for twenty minutes, disparaging the English, sang some songs in his rough, reedy tenor and stumbled off stage. I took him back to the hotel and Beatrice put him to bed.

The next day was December 8, the Feast of the Immaculate Conception, a day when all the bars in Montreal are closed. Except for one: the Montreal Men's Press Club in the old Mount Royal Hotel. Somehow Behan had managed to find it. He had asked a taxi driver where he could get a drink. He was prepared to beard a hostile press corps in their own lair for a drink. Or maybe he enjoyed taunting them.

I found him standing with his back to the bar, a semi-circle of journalists around him. They were buying him drinks, egging him on. The principal of McGill and the proprietor of the *Montreal Star* came into the bar and one of the journalists who wanted to ingratiate himself with such powerful men asked if they would like to meet Brendan Behan. They approached the circle as Behan was in mid-story and waited to be introduced. Behan sensed that these men were of the Establishment and with his unerring sense of mischief, he asked the assembled journalists, in a voice loud enough for everyone to hear, "Who are those fuckin' pricks?"

The two men turned on their heel and walked out of the bar. The next morning there was a scathing editorial in the *Montreal Star* blasting the Irish writer for his boorish behaviour, telling him he was not a welcome guest in the city.

Behan began to drink in earnest. I tried to cut down his intake of whiskey by taking the drinks other people ordered for him and drinking them myself — which was, to say the least, not good for my constitution. I still held on to the faint hope that he would be well enough to appear at the Comédie Canadienne; but the bitterly cold weather, the initial indifference of Montrealers and the hostility of the press combined to sap his energy and his morale. He turned to the bottle for solace and there was nothing that either Beatrice or I could do to stop him.

Needless to say I had to cancel his appearance at the Comédie Canadienne. He became ill and there was concern that he might die in Montreal. All he wanted was to get back to Dublin for Christmas. He took the train back to New York. He would visit Canada again, two years later and this time it would be Toronto's turn to be entertained by the wild Dublin boyo.

After he and Beatrice left, my parents suggested I go away to the Laurentians for a week to "recuperate."

In the solitude of my room at Grey Rocks resort I began to make notes of the week's experience with Brendan Behan. Twelve years later I turned the story into fiction as my first novel, *The Streets of Askelon.*

And I gave up the idea of becoming an impresario.

Cameroon Diary

MARCH 22, 1980. SATURDAY.

The road to Baminda is tarmacked. Women sell green bananas from great bunches at the side of the road on the outskirts of the villages. Bamileke is the name of the tribe who live here, a name given to them by the French. When their country was colonized they were offered deeds to their lands which were respected by the French and the British. They are a tightly-knit people who pool their resources in a co-operative spirit. The women don't marry out of the tribe and as businessmen they are some of the wealthiest in Cameroon. We pass through Mbouda, a Bamileke town. The grass is yellowish up here. The land drier. A mottled effect of browns and greens. Cows are herded on horseback. Vegetables are grown in plots. Approaching the border between East (French-speaking) and West (predominantly English-speaking) Cameroon a large poster advertises the delights of Guinness. An attractive young Cameroonian couple are drinking; she has just poured him a glass. "Discover the secret. Guinness is good for you."

In the North West province the scenery is reminiscent of both the Scottish Highlands and the South Downs. Small wonder the British felt at home here. High rolling hills stippled with rocky outcrops.

Horses and cattle graze on the rolling grasslands. We are out of tse-tse fly country here. Some of the houses are painted the colours of the flag, green, red and yellow. Green windows, red trim, yellow wash. The hump-backed cattle are called Zibou by the French; they are brown, black or silver grey and are tended by the Fulanis. In the grasslands market day is every eighth day — to match the old tradi-tional calender.

MARCH 23, 1980. SUNDAY MORNING.

Met Joseph Lampte, a historian of the Nso people. They live in the English-speaking North of the country. He explained some of the tra-ditions of his clan and then we raced off for a tour of St. Augustine's College where three Canadian teachers are working. After that we went to meet the Fon of Nso, the ruler of the Bui district of Northern Cameroon. Philip Nsai escorted us into the palace, a large stone-built construction with a corrugated iron roof and a series of inner court-yards. The traditional way to approach the Fon, who sat on a carved wooden throne in a blue tie-dyed skirt, black leather zip-up boots and sun glasses, is by blowing into your cupped hands and clapping three times.

The Fon, who speaks five languages, wore a Rolex watch and was very interested in my CBC-issue tape recorder. After a short interview we went into the courtyard to watch the dancing. The Fon has hun-dreds of wives whom he has inherited from his uncle, the former ruler of Nso, and he introduced me to a twelve-year-old girl who would become his next wife.

Mr. Lampte read a speech of welcome on behalf of the Fon which was signed and sealed by the Fon and presented to me: "My distin-guished guest and good friends and members of your entourage, wel-come to the kingdom of Nso and the clan of Nso," it began. "We have come to know you more through the friendship that exists between Canada and Cameroon in general and through the giant water pro-ject made available to the people of this Division by their Canadian friends (a CIDA project). The Canadian staff at St. Augustine's College, Kumbo and the project on equipment given to the College recently amounting to about 700,000 francs CFA are our pride....Do not think that our problems are ended. Look at the extent of my clan: the present water supply covers only about one quarter of immediate area inhabited....I have just been informed that the limited Canadian teaching staff in St. Augustine's College will be reduced. This is a bit unfortunate for us as we have been expecting the fourth member in the staff. The departure of Mrs. Sarah Ryan will now render the Canadian staff in this college short by two. We are, of course, confident that you have designed good plans for this teaching staff. Permit me to request you to convey my personal good wishes and those of my people to your Prime Minister, His Excellency Pierre Trudeau on his re-election as Prime Minister of Canada. The news of his re-election reached us amidst cheers and great jubilation. We are not at all surprised because we knew that he would undoubtedly make it again. We are happy our prayers have been heard. We can now be sure of a continuity in our long standing relations. My people have a saying that the toad's termite does not fly. Such is our position with our friends in Canada...May God be with you throughout your journey back."

... the toad's termite does not fly.

Four of the women dancers were holding live chickens by the feet. Nadine MacDonnell, second secretary at the embassy, whispered to me that these were gifts for me from the Fon. We then went back to the Fon's office to continue the interview. More beer is offered. His son, a young man in his early twenties, approaches and kneels before him. As a mark of favour the Fon holds his hands like a bowl and an aide pours beer into them. The son drinks from his father's hands.

I hear a bleating and a goat is dragged into the room. This is another gift for me from the Fon. He is eyeing my tape recorder. Nadine McDonnell whispers to me that it would be diplomatic for me to present the Fon with my tape recorder.

"This is CBC property," I reply. "I can't just give it away."

"You've got others."

"Yeah, but…"

The thing to do would be to present the Fon with the tape recorder in exchange for the four chickens and the goat.

There was no question that we had to leave with the livestock for fear of creating a diplomatic incident. We tied the chickens' legs together and secured them to the roof rack of the van, along with the long-haired, black-eyed goat.

It was over 100 miles to the next village of Foumban. The sky was darkening and the rain began to fall. The heavens opened and the chickens drowned. The goat, much the worse for wear, could not stand up when we finally reached Foumban. We hired a young boy to look after the sodden goat while we went off for dinner. We instructed him to massage the animal's legs and to exercise him around the town square.

When we returned an hour later the boy was in tears. The goat would not stand up. We gave him 500 francs. He demanded 1000 since he had to carry it around the square. We took the goat to the local nunnery and presented it to them. They were delighted to have it and we to have found a home for it.

I still had one problem. How was I going to explain to the CBC bureaucrats what had happened to the tape recorder?

On my return to Toronto I wrote a long memo explaining the cirumstances — that I had given the tape recorder to the Fon of Nso in exchange for four chickens and a goat. As evidence of this transaction I would have gladly brought the animals back, but the chickens had drowned in a thunderstorm and the goat — well, there are no pasturing possibilities on a 747.

My memo was not acknowledged.

Wine Fairs: Vinexpo

IN THE ENTRANCE TO TORONTO'S EATON CENTRE ON DOWNTOWN Yonge Street is a bronze statue of Timothy Eaton, the founder of the department store chain. The toe of his left shoe is worn to a golden sheen by the myriads of people who have rubbed it over the generations for good luck. (Not that it has worked for the company's current directorate.)

This atavistic gesture of touching or rubbing an image for luck must be a universal need since I have seen statues in Italy with the same shining parts as Timothy Eaton's toe. One is in Florence at the entrance to a covered market square in the centre of the city. It is a large, beautifully executed, life-size bronze replica of a wild boar whose gleaming snout has been polished by the attentions of countless tourists.

The other memorable example is the statue of Shakespeare's Juliet in a courtyard under that celebrated balcony in Verona. The doors, the archway and the walls leading into this courtyard are covered with the names of lovers who no doubt hope for a more felicitous fate than the Bard's Gen-X'ers, Romeo and Juliet.

Juliet stands at the far end of the courtyard, a demure young thing who looks more like a statue of the Madonna, except that her right breast flashes like a beacon in the dimly lit forecourt. Tourists   take turns being photographed fondling her breast. Herein lies the difference between Canadians and Italians. Our basic instincts impel us to touch the toe of an unrepentant capitalist while Italians go for the gusto. I'm sure the French would understand and sympathize: after all, they consider wine to be the liquid embodiment of the female sex.

> *Tourists take turns being photographed fondling her breast. Herein lies the difference between Canadians and Italians.*

While the French and the Italians may agree on some things, their attitudes to wine and wine shows are quite different. Just visit Vinexpo in Bordeaux and Vinitaly in Verona and you can see the differing national attitudes.

Vinexpo happens every other year, in odd years, in June at around the time of flowering if the vintage is good. Vinitaly occurs every year in April.

Vinexpo, while showing off the best that France can provide, also welcomes the world. It is the most international of wine shows; even Ontario and British Columbia wineries feel compelled to have a presence there. Vinitaly invites other wine regions to exhibit but basically it's an Italian event and in Vinexpo years tends to be overshadowed.

Vinexpo is located just outside Bordeaux, the undisputed wine capital of the world (after all, when you think of vintages, your first thought is red Bordeaux). The exhibition hall is a kilometer long, set by the side of an artificial lake. There are ancillary tents along the lakeside for regional and national restaurants (which are uniformly very good and difficult to get into) and other tents and hospitality areas on the other side rented by the large companies.

Invariably it is hot in Bordeaux in June. Blazing hot. And those who were there in 1989 will never forget just how hot. The hall had no air conditioning and the build-up of heat made the place feel like a furnace. Corks rose like magic from the bottles as the alcohol expanded but no one wanted to taste the tepid wines anyway. All we wanted was water. The temperature was said to be 47° Celsius and even hotter in those stands that had an upper deck. There were stories of oysters boiling on the half shell and winemakers collapsing with heart attacks — apocryphal, no doubt, but certainly it was terribly uncomfortable for those who attended. The stands that had their own air-conditioning were much in demand.

My abiding memory of the 1989 Vinexpo will always be the sight of Roberto Anselmi, the fine Soave producer, in shirt sleeves with his trouser legs rolled up to the knees, sitting on the edge of a fountain with his feet dangling in the water. Bags of ice and bottles of his Capitel Foscarino and I Capetelli Soave were also chilling in the makeshift ice bucket.

Many of the châteaux have guests for lunch or dinner during Vinexpo, but an invitation to Mouton-Rothschild is one of the most coveted. It is a black tie event, quite formal. The guests are transported by special train from Bordeaux to the station in Pauillac where they are greeted by the local band and then driven by bus to the château.

That year was my fiftieth birthday and I had been invited to dinner, along with some 200 other guests, to Château Mouton-Rothschild. We lined up on the gravel driveway to be received by Philippine de Rothschild prior to a champagne reception outside and then into the cellars for a candlelit dinner.

I was staying at the Terminus Hotel in Bordeaux which is above the main railway station. It was not air-conditioned and I was forced to sleep with the windows open — which was the lesser of two evils since Vinexpo coincides with La Fête de la Musique when itinerant musicians can perform at all hours of the day and night. Mainly night.

I changed into my tuxedo and took a cab to the smaller local station from which the private train to Mouton was to leave. But the cab driver did not understand my French and took me to a station that was boarded up and abandoned. It did not take me long to realize that I was not going to join the party from there. The train was due to leave in fifteen minutes from a station I had ascertained from a passerby was "*pas loin d'ici.*"

It was blisteringly hot still and I looked around for a passing taxi but the streets in this part of Bordeaux were deserted.

I began to run.

Sweat was pouring off me in buckets. I felt like Niagara Falls. I had five minutes to make the train and I was a good half mile away from the station. I ran faster. My dinner shirt was drenched.

I arrived just as the train was about to pull out of the platform and jumped on board. I might as well have been in a Turkish Bath.

Every pore of my body gave up its fluids. The leather of my shoes felt sodden. My lapels were steaming like a horse that has been ridden hard and put away wet.

Two glasses of champagne helped to cool me down and by the time the train arrived in Pauillac I was merely as hot as the rest of the gathering. In the reception line-up I ran into a fellow Canadian who worked for the Alberta Liquor Board. He had been a wrestler in his youth and when he had taken more wine than a liquor board executive should he was prone to putting head locks on people in bars.

We had drinks on Mouton's terrace and then moved into the cellar for dinner.

The menu read as follows:

Mosaïque légumes au foie gras
Cuisse de canard en civet à l'ancienne
Pâtes au basilic
Fromages
Gourmandise à la vanille au coulis de framboise

The accompanying wines were:

Opus One 1982

Mouton Baron Philippe 1970

Mouton -Rothschild 1939

Sauternes Baronnie 1987

The centrepiece wine, served with the cheese, was the Mouton-Rothschild 1939 in magnums. Since this was my birth year I was over the moon — even though the vintage received no stars at all from Michael Broadbent, who described it in print, having tasted it in May 1978, as "lightish in colour; sound and nice bouquet; with an acceptable twist of acidity."

It hadn't improved in eleven years but it was fun to try. I asked Philippine de Rothschild if she would autograph the label for me, which she graciously did.

The dinner ended about one o'clock; by then the weather had cooled somewhat. We drank cognac on the terrace and my colleague from Alberta approached me, suggesting that I would be better off coming back to his air-conditioned hotel and sleeping there rather than embarking on the long journey back to Bordeaux and the Terminus Hotel. Recalling my sauna-like room and the street music, I decided to take him up on his offer.

... the ideal contraption for soaking labels off wine bottles: a bidet.

He was staying at the Relais de Margaux, a luxury hotel, in a room with twin beds.

It was around two o'clock by the time we arrived back at the hotel. I have no recollection of how we got there. Someone must have driven; I hope it wasn't the Albertan.

I decided at that point that I had to soak the label off the magnum of Mouton 1939. Now the French have invented the ideal contraption for soaking labels off wine bottles: a bidet. I filled the bidet in the hotel bathroom with hot water and then filled the bottle with hot water so that it would lie immersed. The combined heat on both sides of the glass would melt the glue and the label would come away. (This method works for most wine bottles, except those with gold on the label. For some reason gold seems to stick limpet-like to glass.)

It would make a fine momento of Vinexpo 1989.

Mouton's magnum label came away very easily. It measured 6 inches by 4-3/4 inches, slightly larger than the label for a 750 ml bottle; and as a 1939 bottling it bore the Rothschild crest surmounted by a crown and held by two rampant rams. It was not yet an art label (for every vintage since 1945 the late Baron Guy de Rothschild, and latterly his daughter Philippine, have commissioned renowned artists to design the top band of the label. Over the years the works of such luminaries of the art world as Picasso, Chagall, Dali, Miro, Henry Moore, Andy Warhol and Jean-Paul Riopelle have graced that top band.

The design for the 1993 vintage, by Hartung, caused something of a scandal in the States: a pencil drawing of a nude pubescent girl. The Bureau of Alcohol, Tobacco and Firearms, the federal department that polices wine labels (!) was outraged; so Mouton had a special label printed for the US: one with a blank white space in place of the buff-coloured image. This bottling has already become something of a collector's item.)

I placed the 1939 Mouton label lovingly on the flat surface next to the sink and patted it dry with a towel. It would make a fine memento of Vinexpo 1989. The wine of my birth year. By the time I had finished, my room-mate was already in bed, sitting bolt upright.

"Hurry up," he said. "I'm turning out the light."

I undressed quickly and slid into the single bed next to his. The light snapped out and he said, "Good night."

Almost immediately there was the sound of a match being struck and a flame illuminated the room.

"What are you doing?" I demanded.

"Having a smoke," he said. "I always have a smoke before I go to sleep."

"In the dark?"

"Yes."

"I'd rather you didn't."

"Okay," he said, obligingly.

There was the sound of a cigarette being stubbed out in an ashtray and the rustle of sheets as his head hit the pillow. Within seconds he began to snore. Great window-rattling inhalations that pierced through the pillow I used to cover my ears.

After twenty minutes I decided there was no way that I was going to fall asleep with the rolling thunder from the neighbouring bed.

I picked up the pillow and a blanket and walked to the bathroom. The bath itself was too short to sleep in so I made up a bed on the marble floor. Then it occurred to me that the sleeping volcano in the bedroom might want to get up in the night to use the bathroom. I would be in his direct path to the toilet. So I moved sideways until I was positioned under the wash basin and vanity unit. My ear was next to the pipes and when anybody else in the hotel that night flushed a toilet or turned on a tap I was jolted into consciousness by a noise even more devastating than my neighbour's snoring.

"How did you sleep?" he asked me the next morning over breakfast.

"As well as might be expected," I replied. "And you?"

"... I had to use a god-damned wine label."

"Great," he said, "but this morning when I went to the can I couldn't find any toilet paper so I had to use a god-damned wine label."

Wine Fairs: Vinitaly

VINITALY BY COMPARISON TO VINEXPO IS MUCH MORE RELAXED AND slightly chaotic. While Vinexpo takes place in one huge hall, Vinitaly is scattered through a series of halls in an exhibition ground located in an industrial suburb of Verona on Viale del Lavoro (The Avenue of Toil). Anyone who has sat in a traffic jam for over an hour trying to get near the show grounds knows how aptly named this street is.

There is a natural tendency to seek out the winemakers who have become your friends over the years because they will be offended if you don't visit their stands (they know in advance which members of the foreign press are attending the fair and, as with Vinexpo, before you've even left home you receive printed invitations to attend their tastings or at least to drop by). This, of course, means you spend an inordinate amount of time socializing when what you really want to do is to discover what is new and who are the Tiger Woodses of Italian winemakers.

In 1997 I found one: Stephan Inama, a chemical biologist who makes wine in Soave. Inama wines have enormous depth of flavour and will appeal to the North American palate because of their concentration of fruit and their oak treatment. The Inama family own the largest independent estate in Soave and they used to sell their wine to Tedeschi; they also have the oldest Chardonnay planting in the Verona region. Inama make Sauvignon Blanc, Chardonnay, Soave and a dessert wine from Sauvignon Blanc called Vulcaia Après that tastes remarkably like Sauternes.

One of their Soaves comes from grapes they buy in from the Foscarino vineyard, a small volcanic hill in the middle of the Classico region, which also supplies Roberto Anselmi with grapes for his Capitel Foscarino. To my taste, this is the best Soave. No winemaker treats his grapes with more respect than Anselmi. At each stage of fermentation, from the arrival of the grapes in his deceptively large winery, to the crush, the settling of the juice and its passage into the stainless steel tanks, the movements are the gentlest I have seen. The wine is babied into life and the results are clearly there in the bottle.

... he was going two hundred and eighty.

But even more than wine Roberto Anselmi loves speed. He owns three motor bikes and six cars, two of them Porsches. After my visit to the winery, a twenty-minute drive from the fair, he drove me back in his BMW Alpina. On the autostrada he had the car up to 230 km/h. It took half the time but when I entered the grounds of the fair weak at the knees I had to have a grappa at Jacopo Poli's stand to calm my nerves. When I mentioned this to Harvey Steiman of *The Wine Spectator* a couple of weeks later, he said, "That's nothing. I remember driving with Roberto at night back to Verona. And he was going two hundred and eighty."

My favourite wine bar in the world is in Verona. Called La Bottiglia del Vino, it's on a tiny side street just off the Piazza

Erbe. The front part is a bar with stools where you can buy wine by the glass and the back is a restaurant with heavy wooden tables. Bottles line the walls as well as painted inscriptions hymning the praises of wine.

On my maiden trip to Verona in the early 1980s, with three Toronto restaurateurs, I first tasted Quintarelli's amazing Amarone Riserva here. It was Angelo Gaja who ordered it. The original owner of La Bottiglia del Vino had a great respect for winemakers and whenever they entered his premises he would announce them in town crier style, as if they were opera stars.

"Giorgio Grai!"

"Angelo Gaja!"

"Giacomo Bologna!"

All three came in the night I was there and the party just got bigger and bigger.

The late Giacomo Bologna, who did for Barbera what Gaja has done for Barbaresco, was a frequent visitor at La Bottiglia del Vino. Affectionately known as the Pope of Verona, the portly Bologna would come in around midnight and then the festivities would begin. He would head for the basement cellar, sit at the head of the table and tie a serviette around his neck. Dinner would arrive and he would hoover his spaghetti into his mouth as if it were his last meal. Those who dined with him dined well and drank well. The evening I joined him ended up with us pulling bottles from the racks. We left at 4 a.m.

It was in La Bottiglia del Vino that I first saw the trick of cutting the capsule in such a way that you could slide the pulled cork into a ring of lead that was still attached to the neck of the bottle. (With the modern substitutes of tin or plastic instead of the old lead this doesn't work as well. Not everything is progress in the wine world.)

On returning to Toronto after that first visit I wrote an article about the restaurant for *Winetidings* magazine which started this way: "If I die, and as a lover of wine I have no intention of doing

... scatter my ashes on the floor of La Bottiglia del Vino

so, scatter my ashes on the floor of La Bottiglia del Vino…"

The last time I was there I saw the article framed on the wall as you go down to the basement — where ten of us had wined and dined with the Pope of Verona.

*P*iedmont seems to breed showmen. Maybe it's something in the air or something to do with the morning fog that shrouds the hills of the Barolo and Barbaresco regions — the need for sunlight to disperse those damp morning mists. Angelo Gaja has done more to heighten the world's awareness of Barbaresco than anyone else, not only by his superb quality but by his pricing. He is a tireless promoter of his wines and if there were a prize for the world's best dressed vintner it would go to Angelo. He's the most effective model Missoni has.

The embodiment of good taste, Angelo Gaja is a perfectionist in whatever he does. Currently he is renovating an abandoned castle across the road from his winery in Barbaresco to turn it into a hotel, linked by a tunnel to his cellars.

Gaja single vineyard Barbarescos — San Lorenzo, Sori Tildin and Costa Russi — boast the world's longest corks. At a hefty 60 millimeters they defy most corkscrews. Even the Screwpull has difficulty removing them intact.

Angelo has expanded from his home base in Barbaresco into Barolo with his new wine Sperss and across the provincial border into Tuscany. He now owns property in Montepulciano and in Bolgheri (made famous by Sassicaia).

In a Piedmontese village with the delightful name of Cocconato d'Asti, Roberto Bava makes delectable wines. A music lover, he features musical instruments on the labels of his best wines. He told me that over the last three years he had Italy's largest jazz orchestra playing in his cellar. They even made a recording there. The label idea was not just for decoration: "We tried to explain the taste of the wine with the musical sound." The choice was made by the audiences who came to the wine-tasting concerts he put on.

"We had one hundred and fifty in the cellar. Sometimes it was in a theatre or an art gallery and once we did it in a prison. The people listened to the music and then were asked to write their tasting notes."

And what were the findings?

"Statistically, it came out that white wines were more compatible with wind instruments and red wines with stringed instruments. So, the sound of a violin or a cello was more appropriate to a red wine perhaps because both the instrument and the cask are made of wood. And according to the body of the wine it could be large and curved like a bass or a cello.

"On the other hand, white wine is more often a harmonic wine, a cold wine. The sound of brass instruments is colder, more metallic."

Roberto Bava went even further. He asked his audiences what was the music that best explained his wines.

Stravinsky, it seems, is compatible with Gavi, especially "The Rites of Spring" — hence, Bava Gavi features a hunting horn on its label. Mussorgsky's "Pictures From An Exhibition" was recommended for Muscato d'Asti (there's a tuba on the label); for Dvorak's Concerto for Violoncello, a Barbaresco (labelled with a cello); and for the Elephant theme from Saint Saëns' "Carnival of the Animals," the heaviest wine of the region, a Barolo with a double bass on the label. In brief, the musical analogy works this way: loud deep notes, big-bodied wines; high notes, acidic wines.

Bava waxes lyrical when he talks about wine and music: "Paganini explains Barbera because of its elegance. The more Barbera is aged the more it becomes round, maybe going from a vio-lin to a cello. Even bigger if you want. Some Barbera can become a double bass. When we use a special oak for Barbera it becomes some-thing more than a violin — a violin where the wood is very important and where the other decisions of the winemaker are very important. Like a Stradivarius. That's why we call our wood-aged Barbera d'Asti Superiore 'Stradivario.'"

At the 1997 Vinitaly I visited Roberto Bava's stand to taste the 1994 Stradavario. It had a floral, sweet nose with a cherry and licorice taste. The new oak was obvious in the young wine, but the lively acidity and firm tannins augur well for a great wine in a few years.

Bava handed me his expensive Mont Blanc fountain pen to make my notes. The ink was deep purple.

"That's our Barbera d'Asti," he said.

"Why didn't you use your Barolo?" I asked, jokingly.

"I did," he replied. "But it blocked the mechanism. Too much extract."

On Wine Tasting

> ## "The quality of Meursault is not strained."
> ### WILLIAM SHAKESPEARE

Once at a dinner tasting I was conducting at The Old Mill restaurant in Toronto a participant asked the question: "Before I start, should I swallow my gum?"

Experts when addressing lay people always tell their audience, who might be intimidated by the subject matter, that there are no stupid questions.

But sometimes there are.

Public speaking, no matter what the subject, is a matter of confidence. The confidence of the speaker secure in his chosen discipline and the confidence of the audience that the speaker knows what he's talking about and will answer their questions. The best way to establish that bond of trust with an audience is through humour. That's why every speech you will ever hear starts off with a joke to relax the audience (and the speaker, if he or she gets a laugh).

I have two opening gambits that I use, depending on the demographics of the audience.

The first is: "Good evening, ladies and gentlemen. Wine is a very healthy beverage and I am a walking testimonial to its salutary effects. I'm 85 years old."

That usually works as long as I'm not addressing an audience of Generation X's who think I *am* 85 years old or an audience of senior citizens who think I look very good for my age.

The second: "Good evening, ladies and gentlemen. How many people have never been to a wine tasting before?" Given the tentativeness of the response as hands are raised sheepishly you'd think I was asking who was still a virgin. "Good. Now, how many people have not been to a wine tasting since lunch?"

Wine appreciation is rather like choosing a spouse ...

This works well for most audiences except for trade and media affairs where the participants have probably just come from a tasting.

Then I talk about how to assess a wine. "Wine appreciation is rather like choosing a spouse. You're looking for faults first of all. And then when you find you can live with the wine, you can begin praising its virtues."

Wine, as I have said before, is very human. And like us it goes through phases. Exuberant and extrovert when first made, it becomes truculent and uncommunicative in its teenage stage. Wine, like most people, develops character with age. The older it gets the more temperamental it becomes. It doesn't like travel; it can catch cold. When traumatized (at bottling) it closes in on itself. All very human traits.

Just as human beings have different personalities, so do wines. And we react to wines according to our own conditioning and preferences. What a boring world it would be if we all liked the same wine. All we would need is a United Nations Red and United Nations White.

We all taste through our own cipher. This cipher is part of our cultural-anthropological baggage — how and where we were brought up and what taste experiences we have been conditioned to enjoy. The Portuguese and the Chileans like what we consider to be oxidized white wines. The English, as I have mentioned, prize geriatric champagne. Germans, in spite of the Trocken trend (wines made in bone-dry style) really prefer their wines to have some residual sweetness. The French tend to drink their wines young, the Australians love oak, and the Italians have yet to come to terms with the fact that they also make *white* wine.

These are gross generalizations, of course, but time and again I find national preferences are reinforced at tastings.

On March 1, 1990, Steven Spurrier (whose name will live in infamy among the Bordelais as the villain who set up that famous taste-off in Paris between Californian Cabernet Sauvignon and top-flight red Bordeaux in 1976. California won hands down) held a Bordeaux tasting of the 1970 vintage in Toronto. Virtually all the participants, experienced Canadian tasters, chose Château Lynch-Bages as their favourite wine. It was wonderfully concentrated with sweet blackcurrant fruit. Spurrier himself preferred the Château Montrose, a notoriously tannic wine from the commune of St. Estèphe. To my palate this wine was lean and closed and needed much more time to develop.

Those who chose the Lynch-Bages were tasting through a North American palate used to the bright, up-front fruit of Californian and New World wines. Spurrier was tasting through the cipher of the London wine trade whose long association with and affection for claret has made them appreciate the more austere wines. The North American palate, by contrast, revels in fat, juicy wines that offer instant gratification. (Rather like North American football which, like most American sports, including baseball, is based on the orgasm — short, sharp, explosive action followed by long moments of tedium.)

This same palate syndrome was brought home to me when I was a judge at the *Dallas Morning News* National Wine Competition in January 1996. My three fellow panelists were from Texas and California. On the first day of the competition we had to blind-taste 112 American Merlots, retaining only those we wanted to retaste the next day. When it came to the medal round I found myself dissenting from my colleagues in many cases because, having learned my wine in England, my yardstick for a fine Merlot was Pomerol rather than Washington or Napa Valley.

And this is the reason I never rate wines by number. I hope that I will not have to eat my words since more and more publications are going over to the number system. I must admit I choose my movies this way. If a reviewer's taste in films coincides with my own, I make a point of seeing anything he or she accords four stars. Yet the analogy does not work when it comes to wine. Once it is made, a film, like a can of beans, does not change unless it is re-cut. Our response to films is emotional and intellectual. Wines we appreciate through our senses and these change according to our mood, our health and the environment in which we are tasting. Our palate perceives a wine differently at 9 a.m. in a laboratory than it does over the dinner table with friends or outdoors on the patio. If we have a cold or are feeling under the weather we are not going to have the same sensory acuity as we would if we were well.

So, if I were to give a wine a number having tasted it, my evaluation would be very specific but only for the time and the circumstances under which I tasted it. I might find a wine that has been recently bottled and is suffering from bottle shock (tight and closed). If I give that wine 76 out of 100 then that wine will always be a 76 unless my notes accompany it, saying: "This Chardonnay is rather dumb at the moment, not showing much on the nose, but the flavours are there and with a little bottle age it will develop into a beautifully balanced and harmonious wine. 76/100 at the moment." Then again I might praise an old wine and give it 91/100. Wine merchants or advertisers may take my number and use it two years after I wrote my notes when the wine has begun to lose its fruit and is no longer a 91.

Which leads me to a confession. I have come to a point in my life when I don't fully trust people who don't like wine. Those who shun the fermented grape for medical reasons I can understand, but those who reject wine out of hand — well, frankly I'd rather seek my companionship elsewhere.

... I don't fully trust people who don't like wine.

Why, you might ask, would I spurn vast segments of society because they don't like wine? Let me put it this way: I would rather spend my time with those who do. I have found that people who enjoy wine are in the main extraordinarily generous and would rather share a great bottle with you than hoard it for themselves.

One of the most generous wine lovers I have encountered is a retired commodities broker who puts on amazing tastings in Chicago. His name is Stephen A. Kaplan and we are both on the Advisory Board of The Masters of Wine for North America. On April 11 and 12, 1997, he organized a Wine and Food Weekend which consisted of three events: Red Bordeaux from the 1982 vintage, accompanying dinner, at the Four Seasons Hotel; Mature Champagne Veuve Clicquot Ponsardin accompanying lunch at the Ritz Carlton Hotel; and Wines from the Year 1947 accompanying dinner at Les Nomades restaurant. One of the guests flew in from Belgium to be there.

Before we sat down to thirty-two 1982 clarets, we drank Dom Pérignon 1982 to lay the dust of travel. The wines were arranged in flights as follows:

1. Beychevelle, Calon-Ségur, Grand-Puy-Lacoste, La Lagune (magnum), Léoville-Barton, Léoville-Poyferré (magnum).
2. Canon (magnum), Ducru-Beaucaillou, Figeac, Gruaud-Larose, Palmer, Pavie

3. Certan-de-May, L'Évangile, La Conseillante, Latour à Pomerol, Trotanoy.
4. Cos d'Estournel, La Mission-Haut-Brion, Léoville-Las-Cases, Lynch-Bages, Pichon-Longueville Comtesse de Lalande.
5. Ausone (magnum), Cheval-Blanc, Lafleur, Pétrus, Le Pin.
6. Latour, Mouton-Rothschild, Haut-Brion, Margaux, Lafite.

The final flight of First Growths was served blind and the twenty-one of us at table had to determine the order. Haut-Brion as a Graves is easy to spot. The wine has a slightly medicinal character rather like iodine or seaweed. Latour and Mouton are both huge wines with high Cabernet Sauvignon content. In this vintage I have always found Mouton to be sweeter and less "cigar box." Once I had sorted these out it was a matter of deciding between Margaux and Lafite. The Lafite was tight and tannic while the Margaux was creamy and soft. I got them right.

I may have been able to recognize blind the five First Growth Bordeaux of the 1982 vintage but I have also got it wrong more often than not. Let me tell you about my induction into the Cofradia de Caballeros de San Miguel de las Vinas. This is a Spanish wine order along the lines of the Chevaliers des Tastevin in Burgundy. As part of the ceremony, which involves robes and funny hats that look like toques, you have to drink a glass of water and smash the glass, forswearing water, drink from a glass decanter with a spout that resembles an ancient wine skin, and identify a rosé and a white wine blindfolded — all of this in front of a large audience.

Miguel Torres was the master of ceremonies and the two glasses of wine he handed me were both at room temperature. I tasted the one in my left hand. It had the flavour of wild strawberries, a dead giveaway for rosé.

I got it wrong.

The crowd groaned.

"Taste them again," Miguel whispered. "Both of them."

I began to sweat. I tasted each glass. My taste buds had closed down in panic. By this time I could not tell a Chardonnay from fish and chips. But I had a fifty-fifty chance whichever glass I chose as the white wine. My reputation as a wine writer was on the line. I took a wild guess and raised my left hand.

> *... I could not tell a Chardonnay from fish and chips.*

Applause, applause. I was right.

Now I know why contestants on TV game shows can suddenly "freeze" and have a mental block over a seemingly easy question.

The wine industry has produced some very flamboyant characters who have captured the imagination of wine lovers as much by their antics as by the quality of their wine. I offer you my favourites whose zaniness is allied to a shrewd promotional mind.

1. Walter Taylor of New York's Bully Hill who believes hybrids are the future and keeps alive an ancient battle to use his name on his labels.
2. Stephen Cypes of Summerhill Estate Winery in British Columbia who ages his sparkling wine under a thirty-foot-high pyramid in the vineyard and really believes it makes a difference.
3. Randall Grahm of Bonny Doon in Santa Cruz, the Rhône Ranger, who is quick with a pun and has the most fun with his labels. His Big House Red's back label reads like a ransom note.
4. John Paul of Cameron in Oregon whose winery newsletter deserves a wider audience — it's a scream.

My top favourite, however is, Willi Opitz, the Barnum and Bailey of Austrian wine.

Willi's philosophy: "A winemaker maybe has thirty-five possibilities to make a great wine, then your life is gone."

I first met Willi Opitz in Bordeaux at Vinexpo in the hot year of 1989. He had a tiny booth among the Austrian producers' stand, yet there were crowds of wine writers and foreign winemakers around him. He let me try his extraordinary dessert wines with their intense perfumes which he was pouring liberally for anyone who came within range. As a memento of my visit — as if the memory of the wines weren't enough — he gave me a small plastic case: it contained one inch of rusted barbed wire. A piece of history. It was a strand of barbed wire that had been strung along the top of the Berlin Wall.

Willi is a mechanical engineer who happens to make wine off five hectares of vines (three of them rented) near the Hungarian border. His vineyard site is a thirty-minute drive south of Vienna in the town of Illmitz opposite Rust, on the west bank of the Neusiedlersee. This shallow, reed-filled lake evaporates in late summer to produce humid conditions ideal for the generation of botrytis. And this is what Willi Opitz specializes in: botrytized wines of intense sweetness — although he also makes wines in drier styles.

He produced his first Beerenauslese wine in 1975, not from customary white grapes but from the red Blaufränkisch, a quirky style he has made his own. When his fruit failed to ripen sufficiently, he borrowed a trick from the older winemakers in Rust and left the bunches to dry for three months before pressing on reeds gathered from the lake. Hence the name he coined in 1989, *Schilfmandl*, a wine that features on its label a small bird that lives in the Neusiederlersee reeds.

In 1991 Willi Opitz made his first Trockenbeerenauslese (TBA) wine also from a red variety, Blauburgunder. Then he tried other reds for TBA quality, Zweigelt and Blaufränkisch. "I thought let's do something new, let's make botrytis wines from red grapes, from a different country," he will tell you, using the present tense as if the story has yet to unfold.

No one else makes red TBA, he will tell you with evident relish. "The Beerenauslese I make is barely blush in colour but the
TBA is as deep as a red wine. Everybody said to me you have to
protect your red grapes from botrytis because it kills the colour.
We press everything immediately to avoid rot. From
Beerenauslese grapes you get about 50 per cent of the normal
juice when you press the bunches. So the ratio of liquid in the
grape to skin colour is high. If you have a Trockenbeerenauslese
you have only 10 to 12 per cent liquid in the grape but you have
the same skin colour. In this case the proportion is positive for
the colour so it's darker. We're proud to have something new for
the wine portfolio. Our mission," says Willi, warming to his
theme, "is to make unique and innovative wines like the
Schilfmandl or the red botrytis wine we call Opitz One." (Robert
Mondavi has yet to comment.)

Perhaps Willi Opitz got his taste for sweet wines from his years
working for the American company that markets Mars bars and
M&M candies in Europe. Whatever the motivation he is a cease-
less experimenter. From last year's harvest Willi Opitz made a
Trockenbeerenauslese of Cabernet Sauvignon grapes he bought in
from a neighbour. He has one barrel and he's going to call the
wine Opitz Two.

Ever on the look-out to promote his tiny but expensive production, Willi Opitz met the Formula One racing car driver Ron
Dennis of the McLaren team at the opening of the Hotel du Vin
in England. The two men hit it off and decided to make wine
together.

This unlikely collaboration has spawned a new Opitz label:
McLaren Formula Wine.

In 1996 Willi Opitz made a mere 25,000 half bottles of wines
ranging from dry to sticky — from Muskat Ottonel Spätlese
Trocken to Weslchriesling Beerenauslese to Welschriesling
Eiswein and TBAs of Grüner Veltliner and Scheurebe, as well as
his red dessert wines. Showman that he is, the quality of the wine
is reflected in the packaging. "Every bottle of Opitz One is hand-

signed," says Willi. "I have a gold pen that I use to sign Opitz One 1993, Willi Opitz, with just a small back label. Instead of numbering each bottle we put our fingerprint on the bottle to make it unique."

"Life's too short to waste it on bad wine."

Unique too are the labels that decorate his other wines, delicate water colours painted by his graphic artist brother-in-law Jobst Teltschik. His brushes are wetted with the actual wines rather than water before dipping into the paints. Parts of a painting he did for the brochure to launch the McLaren Formula Wine grace the labels of the 1994 Welschriesling, 1994 Late Harvest Muskat Ottonel and 1994 Scheurebe Trockenbeerenauslese, sold as a boxed selection. Under Willi's logo at the end of that brochure is the injunction, "Life's too short to waste it on bad wine."

Willi believes that you should experience his wines with all the senses. Apart from the organoleptic pleasures they offer and the visual appeal of the artwork and the slender glass bottles, he has gone one step further and recorded the sound of their fermentation on a CD. You can hear fourteen tracks of gurglings and bubblings that would make John Cage proud. The curious thing is that they all sound different! I never did listen to the whole CD through, because it has as soporific an effect as the wine.

"Listen to it," Willi told me, "and you can change your living room into a wine cellar."

He should market the disc as a substitute for Melatonin.

When you think of Riesling your mind turns naturally to the Rhine and Mosel valleys. But Austria makes great Rieslings too; so do New Zealand and Ontario. These wines are shamefully under-appreciated today. Why, oh why has the world turned its back on Riesling? For all Riesling's virtues, the consuming public ignores it and flocks to Chardonnay, Sauvignon Blanc and Pinot Gris instead.

As a grape variety Riesling makes some of the best bone dry wines on this planet, some of the finest dessert wines, and every shade of sweetness in between. With its fine spine of acidity and spicy complexity it is the most versatile of wines for matching with cuisines as diverse as French, Mexican, Thai and Californian.

No dry white wine, with the possible exception of Chenin Blanc from the Loire, ages as long or as beautifully as Riesling. A Schloss Schönborn Johannisberger Vintage 1735 from the Rheingau was opened a few years ago and found to be still alive and drinking well. Not that I'm advocating that you leave your Riesling to mature for 250 years; but don't worry if you neglect it in your cellar for a decade or two.

A chef in the Vosges Mountains once told me that the dry Riesling of his native Alsace was like "a naked sword." The simile is apt. At its best, Riesling from cool climate growing regions has a brightness in the glass, a racy crispness and a mouth-freshening brilliance of citrus and floral flavours like no other wine. It is clean and long and shining just like a sword. Naked, because it is unadorned. What you get from the vineyard is what you have to work with in the cellar. You can't cosmetically improve Riesling by fancy vinting techniques or disguise its flaws with overpowering oak flavours.

Chardonnay, by comparison, is a compliant hussy of a grape. Anyone can grow it and if you slap enough make-up on it (new oak) and rough it up in the barrel (lees stirring) you're going to make a presentable wine. Riesling is uncompromising: what's in the grape is what you get. Putting it another way, Riesling is a sculpture chiselled out from a block of stone; Chardonnay is a sculpture you build up by accreting clay on clay. There is no room for error in Riesling; Chardonnay you can fudge.

Next time you're at a wine tasting, look around you. Notice how many people are left-handed. I guarantee that you will find substantially more than 10 per cent of the room write with the left hand.

From my personal observation over the years I have found that there is a disproportionate number of lefties in the wine trade and among those who are serious amateurs. I myself am left-handed and so are one-third of the members of the Toronto chapter of The Wine Writers' Circle. The generally accepted statistic on left-handed people in the world is 10 per cent. The number of left-handed wine buffs by my calculation runs between 25 and 30 per cent.

Maybe it has something to do with the predominance of the right brain, the hedonistic side. But then, Terry Robards, Senior Managing Editor of *The Wine Enthusiast*, told me that the number of American wine writers born in the month of November is out of all proportion to those born in the other eleven months.

You'd think somehow that the sign of the bull would be more appropriate than that of the scorpion. After all, that's how Dionysus manifested himself to his followers.

Wine & Literature

> "I like wine. It gets me drunk."
> ERNEST HEMINGWAY

*O*f all members of the Fifth Estate the most relaxed and convivial group are the wine writers. Small wonder, do I hear you say? Perhaps. But we happy band of writers on the fringe of journalism come by our calling honestly since we all have a (literally) consuming passion for our subject and generally we have to badger our editors into carrying a wine column in the first place.

Most wine writers have other jobs. Very few can support themselves by wine writing alone. And most of those I have met are, coincidentally, creative in other fields of writing. But then, Dionysus was not only the god of wine, but the god of drama as well.

I am not saying that only writers really enjoy wine, but they cannot resist the temptation to share their interest and knowledge with their readers. While they may be circumspect about revealing other details of their private lives, they seem only too willing to declare themselves (come out of the cellar?) concerning their love of wine.

Colette wrote, in *Prisons et Paradis*: "Between my eleventh and fifteenth year I drank Château Lafite, Chambertin and Corton which had escaped capture by the Prussians in 1870," served by a mother concerned that she was outgrowing her strength. She recalls having had her first glass of wine at the age of three — a Muscat de Frontignan.

Ford Madox Ford began his wine drinking career somewhat later. He drank his first French wine when he was eight but he did not share Colette's taste for sweet wines. He was not enamoured of "the disgusting treacle they call Château Yquem."

Robert Louis Stevenson was less critical: "I am interested in all wines and have been all my life, from the raisin wine that a school-fellow kept secreted in his playbox up to my latest discovery, those notable Valtellinas, that once shone upon the board of Caesar...."

You can tell if someone likes wine merely by the way he or she writes about it. Homer, Shakespeare, Rabelais, Byron and Beaudelaire must have been engaging drinking companions. Each singled out a specific wine for praise. Keats in "Ode to a Nightingale" has the best description of champagne I have read: "…beaded bubbles winking at the brim." Thackeray shared the poet's affection for this sparkling wine — and in copious quantities. "A man who offers champagne by driblets," he wrote, "is a fellow who would…screw on spurs to his boots to make believe he had a horse." Charles Lamb would have pounded the table in agreement with that sentiment if he hadn't already been under it. In his biography of that great English essayist, E. V. Lucas records the sight of Lamb being carried like a sack of potatoes from the dining room, singing, "diddle, diddle, dumpling, my son John" at the top of his voice.

There is also a kind of literary posturing, an inverted snobbery which leads writers to denigrate the source of their inspiration. In Disraeli's novel *Sybil*, Mr. Mountchesney says, "I rather like bad wine. One gets so bored with good wine." One of Anthony Burgess's characters refers to wine-worship as "the most vulgar of idolatries."

The British thriller writer Gavin Lyall had this advice on serving wine in a bed-sitter: "Always match the drinks to the colour of the carpet."

> **"Always match the drinks to the colour of the carpet."**

Marcel Proust was a frightful snob, especially in matters oenological. He has Monsieur Swann send a case of Asti Spumante to Aunts Celine and Flora at the suggestion of "one of the smartest members of the Jockey Club, a particular friend of the Comte de Paris and the Prince of Wales." The assumption was that this sweet, fizzy wine would be just the ticket for two elderly maiden aunts living in the country.

Name dropping is another form of snobbery, especially when you get it wrong. Ian Fleming made Taittinger Blanc de blancs champagne famous in his James Bond novels, but he committed the ultimate faux pas when he referred to Dom Pérignon 1946. There is no such vintage. He also called Piesporter Goldtröptchen a Rhine wine when in fact it comes from the Middle Mosel.

In 1935 Hilaire Belloc wrote a manuscript called *Advice* for the daughter of a family friend who was getting married. The book, with his original drawings of corkscrews, wine funnel and bottle rack, counselled the young bride on matters of wine and food. The slim volume was subsequently published in 1960 with a short introduction by Evelyn Waugh. "[Belloc's] interest in food, wine and domestic matters," wrote Waugh, "was strong and idiosyncratic to the verge of perversity."

One of Belloc's tips is how to remove a stubborn cork from a champagne bottle: "The rule is to take a sharp knife and cut off the excrescence leaving the rest of the cork flush with the top of the bottle. Then pull it out as you would an ordinary cork." (Unless you want to dislocate your shoulder, do not, under any circumstances, try to open a bottle of champagne in this manner. The gas in a bottle of champagne creates a pressure of 90 lbs per square inch — in other words, the pressure of a bus tire. Unimpeded, the cork will leave the bottle at a speed of 65 kms per hour.)

Nor is there any guarantee that a love of wine will produce great literature from writers and poets better known even than Hilaire Belloc. Perhaps the most excruciatingly bad poetry ever written in praise of wine came from the pen of Henry Wadsworth Longfellow. The poem was called "Catawba Wine," after a grape whose most endearing quality is that it produces wines in various shades of pink.

I reproduce here two of its eleven stomach-clutching stanzas:

> For richest and best
> Is the wine of the West,
> That grows by the Beautiful River;
> Whose sweet perfume
> Fills all the room
> With a benison on the giver.
>
> Very good in its way
> Is the Verzenay,
> Or the Sillery soft and creamy;
> But Catawba wine
> Has a taste more divine,
> More dulcet, delicious, and dreamy.

Ernest Hemingway, whose prose was terse and clipped in his novels, became positively expansive and maudlin when he wrote about wine, especially in his bull-fighting book, *Death In The Afternoon*.

Wine is one of the most civilized things in the world and one of the natural things of the world that has been brought to the greatest perfection, and it offers a greater range of enjoyment and appreciation, than possibly any other purely sensory thing that may be purchased....I would rather have a palate that will give me the pleasure of enjoying completely a Château Margaux or a Haut Brion...even though excesses indulged in in the acquiring of it have brought a liver that will not allow me to drink Richebourg, Corton or Chambertin, than to have the corrugated internals of my boyhood when all red wines were bitter except port and drinking was the process of getting down enough of anything to make you feel reckless.

Hardly vintage Hemingway when it comes to prose styling but I can empathize with him.

Evelyn Waugh, who chronicled his youthful wine excesses in *Brideshead Revisited*, preferred port in his later years but was painfully aware of its anatomical effects in those who are prone to gout. He warned that port was not a drink for "the very young, the vain and the active."

I have always thought of Waugh as the reincarnation of Jonathan Swift. The author of *Gulliver's Travels* drank wine mainly for medicinal purposes at the end of his life. A bottle of French wine a day was "the only thing that keeps me out of pain," he wrote. "I am thrifty in everything but wine."

Charles Dickens liked port; Max Beerbohm favoured Valpolicella as his house wine; Arnold Bennett preferred Burgundies; and Friedrich Engels's idea of a good time was Margaux 1848 — which shows a remarkably elevated palate for a man of the people. Voltaire had a fascist streak when it came to the enjoyment of his cellar. He served Louis Latour Côte de Beaune to his friends but kept that shipper's Volnay for himself. This story has a modern echo in the behaviour of the former President of the United States, Richard Milhouse Nixon. In their

Why waste a great wine?

book on Watergate, *Washington Post* investigative reporters Woodward and Bernstein recorded that Nixon would entertain his southern senator cronies on his yacht, the *Sequoia*, moored in New York harbour. He ordered his staff to serve his guests "a rather good six-dollar bottle [while] his glass was to be filled from a bottle of Château Margaux 1966 wrapped in a towel."

The man had a mania for cover-ups. But I can understand his thought process. Nixon appreciated fine wine. Those southern senators would have sat down to dine with their palates anaesthetized with Bourbon. They would be in no condition to enjoy a Château Margaux 1966 even if they understood what they were being served. Why waste a great wine? Save it for those who will appreciate it.

The last place I lived in London before returning to Canada in 1976 was a flat in Neville Court on Abbey Road, directly across from The Beatles' recording studio. In fact, if you study the cover of their Abbey Road album (the four lads are crossing the road on what the British graphically call a zebra crossing) you can see the Victorian red-brick apartment block on the right hand side. My apartment, which was large enough for my daughter Annabel to cycle around in on her tricycle at the age of three, was on the ground floor of the building, or rather slightly underground since we had to go downstairs to the front door.

With the success of The Beatles, the EMI studio became something of a shrine for Beatle lovers. The Abbey Road street sign was forever disappearing and Scandanavian tourists were forever being knocked down by on-coming traffic when they tried to emulate that famous album cover photograph.

I had first met The Beatles in March 1963. As the pop reporter for *Radio Times* I was assigned to cover a concert at the Albert Hall featuring several emerging groups: The Dave Clark Five, Gerry and The Pacemakers and, I believe, Herman's Hermits were on the bill. The Beatles had just come down to London from Liverpool and no one had heard much about them. Although I was the pop reporter I knew very little about rock 'n' roll, certainly not enough to evaluate raw, new talent. So I invited along a teenage actress who was appearing as a panelist on a BBC-TV music show that voted newly released pop records a "Hit" or a "Miss". Her name was Jane Asher. Her brother Gordon had his own group, Peter & Gordon, and their father was a Harley Street psychiatrist.

Scandanavian tourists were forever being knocked down by on-coming traffic...

The only group Jane Asher really responded to in that concert was The Beatles and she said she would like to meet them. During the intermission we made our way down to the bowels of the Albert Hall where the group was changing in a space that looked like the changing room of a rather seedy health club.

Ringo was the first to respond to the beautiful Titian-haired young actress.

"Do you want to go to a party?" he asked her right off the bat in his heavy Liverpool accent.

"I'm sorry?" said Jane, in her very genteel, finishing school accent.

"A party. Do you want to go?"

Thinking of work the next morning, I bowed out. After the concert Jane left with The Beatles. I wish I'd gone along with them.

My then sister-in-law lived with us in the Abbey Road flat. She worked for Abbey National, a building society whose office in

Baker Street occupied the site of Sherlock Holmes's fictional chambers at Number 221B. Abbey National employs a full-time secretary whose job it is to answer all the mail that is sent to Sherlock Holmes at that address.

In 1986 I was asked to deliver a paper by The Bootmakers of Toronto, Canada's National Sherlockian society — "a literary fellowship devoted to Sherlock Holmes, his place in the genre of criminous literature and the works of Sir Arthur Conan Doyle." They were holding a four-day colloquium at the University of Toronto's Trinity College. This was a serious affair; the titles of some of the fourteen papers smacked of PhD theses: "Sherlock Holmes: the consulting detective as modernist critic," "A Study In Scarlet: Canonical theme and structure," "Sherlock Holmes as the mythic hero."

I had read most of Conan Doyle's stories of the great detective when I was at school and I recall how baffled I was when I read that one of his villains was fifty-one years of age. At the tender age of thirteen I thought this was far too old to bear malice toward anyone.

The man who invited me to deliver the paper styled himself in the programme as "Lewis David St. C. Skene-Melvin, B.A., B.L. Sc., M.Phil., M.Bt., B.S.I., one-time librarian and intellectual manqué. A founder-member of The Bootmakers of Toronto, founder of The Sub-Librarians' Scion of The Sherlock Holmes Society of London within the Canadian Library Association, invested in the Baker Street Irregulars as The Duke of Holdernesse, and Mr. Meyers for 1985, Col. Skene-Melvin is fortunately married to Ann Rothery Skene-Melvin, M.A., M.L.S., A.S.H., proprietress of Ann's Books and Mostly Mysteries; otherwise, he'd be insufferable."

The title of the paper made me feel I was back at graduate school, but this one I was determined to finish: "Wine in the Canon in relation to late Victorian oenological tastes, fashions and fads." In order to write it I had to reread the series of Holmes stories and novels. This was more fun than I had anticipated and here is what I wrote, having combed the oeuvre for references to beverage alcohol:

First I would like to set the scene regarding the drinking habits of Holmes and Dr.Watson. As late as 1858 beer was drunk for breakfast by farmers and labourers and was also the beverage of choice among students and under-graduates. When Queen Victoria ascended the throne wine in middle class households invariably meant port or sherry. In Mrs. Beeton's *Complete Etiquette for Gentlemen*, published in 1876, the arbiter of taste stated that "sherry is *the* dinner wine." The nearest the middle classes got to drinking table wine were the homemade country wines fermented from fruits, flowers and vegetables. These were invariably alcoholic and potent. Red currant was regarded as a lady's wine because of its rich sweetness. Gooseberry, by contrast, resembled champagne in its briskness, if not its flavour.

> ... wine in middle class households invariably meant port or sherry.

Professor George Saintsbury, the Oxford don who wrote a history of the French novel, was the author of a seminal work, *Notes On A Cellarbook*. This small volume, published in 1920, was to influence a whole generation of wine writers even though it looked back to the wines of the Edwardian era. On the subject of country wines Saintsbury wrote: "Raisin wine can be doctored into something not unlike coarse Tent (a Spanish red from Alicante): and "orange" into something by no means distantly suggestive of sherry and bitters. But all these are amiable "faking," brandy being the chief accessory after the fact. Currant is a poor creature ... and as for "cowslip," I should wish it kept for less Arcadian Arcadia. Of elder wine, though it need not be actually and immediately nasty, I am bound to say that, when I think of it, I always think likewise of the West Indian prelate who related his experience with some hospitable members of his flock. "They gave me," he said, "some wine — very nice wine; and then some cigars — very nice cigars. I think that, later, we had some rum — very nice rum. But, do you know that afterwards I was positively ILL.""

If the middle classes's acquaintance with wine was largely based on what they could pluck from the field and the hedgerow, the upper classes had their claret and their port. Port had been a favourite since the Methuen Act of 1703 slapped a prohibitive tax on the wines of France. But even when England was at war with its traditional enemy across the channel there was enough red Bordeaux in the cellars of country gentlemen to tide them over until peace was restored and wine imports began again.

The aristocracy did have one particularly revolting drink: toast soaked in boiling water. The result was left till it cooled, strained and then consumed at lunch and dinner with the cheese course. This custom did not die out until the end of the nineteenth century. Mercifully.

Champagne was popular in late Victorian times and by 1870 the fashion was for dry as opposed to sweet champagne. It was consumed with the meal and followed with claret for the dessert course. In Edwardian times, port became the dessert wine.

Dining out in London was the accepted custom by the turn of the century and the typical meal in the grand style might be this one — taken from Saintsbury's *Notes on A Cellarbook*.

First course: clear soup served with sherry

Second course: fried trout, again with sherry

Third course: filets de boeuf and roast duckling served with vintage champagne

Dessert course: apricots à la Rosebery served with port (in this case Cockburn's 1881) and then grilled sardines followed by coffee and Green Chartreuse.

From 1893 Londoners could buy wines from Texas, Australia and California as well as European wines. The Edwardians drank their wines at much the same temperatures as we do today.

In preparing this paper I re-read the entire body of Sherlock Holmes stories specifically looking for references to wine and food. I was curious to see how much Sir Arthur Conan Doyle knew about wine and to what extent he used wine or any other alcoholic beverage in the plot mechanism. In *A Study In Scarlet*, when Watson first meets Holmes, he is fascinated by the great detective's intellectual limitations as well as his abilities. At one point he enumerates them: "Knowledge of literature — nil. Knowledge of philosophy — nil. Knowledge of Astronomy — nil. Knowledge of Politics — feeble. Knowledge of Botany — Variable."

Dr. Watson could have added: Knowledge of wine — virtually nil." And that, from having read the sum total of the novels and short stories, would go for Conan Doyle too. Watson, that most decent of Englishmen, has a more robust if equally ill-informed approach to matters oenological. At least he is on the side of the angels. In *The Sign of the Four* Watson tackles Holmes on his drug dependence. "Whether it was the Beaune which I had taken with my lunch or the additional exasperation produced by the extreme deliberation of his manner, I suddenly felt that I could hold out no longer. "Which is it today," I asked, "morphine or cocaine?"

Holmes showed little interest in wine.

Drugs and wine are incompatible, which may be why Holmes showed little interest in wine. But he does like whisky.

At the end of the novel, Holmes invites Athelney Jones to have a whisky and soda. And the final words of the chapter are, "...I insist upon your dining with us. It will be ready in half an hour. I have oysters and a brace of grouse, with something a little choice in white wines. To Watson: "You have never recognized my merits as a housekeeper."

The point is that Holmes never identifies the wines he speaks of, whereas Watson will at least mention the region.

Holmes carries a flask of whisky which he offers Jonathan Small when they capture him and a whisky and water when he has told his grisly tale.

Whisky is obviously Holmes's preferred drink. In *Scandal in Bohemia* we find Holmes and Watson talking in the early hours of the morning over a glass of whisky and soda in their Baker Street digs.

Men of rank and status equal to Sherlock Holmes are offered whisky on social occasions or when they are in distress or overwrought. While social inferiors, like the engineer whose thumb is cut off, and outright villains like James Ryder, who stole the Blue Carbuncle, are offered a brandy and water or neat brandy to revive them. Women, on the other hand, are offered a glass of wine. In *The Man with the Twisted Lip* Watson's wife offers her friend Kate Whitney wine and water.

Holmes himself is not above taking a dash of spirits when he feels run down. In *The Reigate Squires* he calls for brandy. "My strength," he says, "has been rather tired of late."

If Conan Doyle knew little of wine, he was aware of renowned vintages. In *The Stockbroker's Clerk*, Watson describes the expression on Holmes's face: "like a connoisseur who had just taken his sip of a Comet vintage." Interestingly enough he doesn't say *the* Comet vintage — the miraculous 1811; he is subscribing to the superstition that whenever a comet is sighted the wines of that year will be superlative. This is not the case.

Conan Doyle was minimally more interested in food than he was in wine, if his literary references are any guide, and his favourite meal would appear to be breakfast. We are treated to some fulsome descriptions of what Holmes and Watson (the original Odd Couple) had for their first meal of the day — more so than any other. But then the English have always excelled at breakfast. In *The Naval Treaty* is this description: "The table was laid and just as I was about to ring, Mrs. Hudson entered with the tea and coffee. (Coffee, incidentally, seems to be a habit Holmes picked up on the Continent. References to it began appearing in stories following his Reichenbach hiatus.) A few minutes later she brought in the covers and we all drew up to the table, Holmes ravenous, I curious and Phelps in the gloomiest state of depression.

Holmes and Watson (the original Odd Couple) ...

"Mrs. Hudson has risen to the occasion," said Holmes, uncovering a dish of curried chicken. "Her cuisine is a little limited, but she has as good an idea of breakfast as a Scotsman. What have you there, Watson?"

"Ham and eggs," I answered.

"Good! What are you going to take, Mr. Phelps? Curried fowl, eggs, or will you help yourself?"

"Thank you, I can eat nothing," said Phelps."

Holmes presses him and when Phelps lifts the cover underneath is the missing naval treaty. A rotten trick to play on anyone first thing in the morning. Phelps had to be kept from fainting by having brandy poured down his throat.

Even when Conan Doyle takes his hero to Lausanne, as happens in *The Disappearance of Lady Frances Carfax*, we get no mention of food whatsoever in this centre of Swiss gastronomy.

Eggs are the only dish which Holmes ever discusses in terms of their preparation. But even this single reference to cuisine shows little interest in matters of the kitchen. In *The Problem of the Bridge*, the detective ruminates, "Even so trivial a matter as cooking an egg demands an attention which is conscious of the passage of time." Not exactly a recipe for a four-minute egg.

Yet Holmes does have a predilection for eggs. In *The Valley of Fear* he demolishes four boiled eggs and toast for high tea, and his preferred breakfast is two boiled eggs (sometimes scrambled) and toast. Although he is not above smoking his pipe before a meal as he does in *The Valley of Fear* and *The Engineer's Thumb*. And he smokes a cigarette before breakfast in *The Hound of the Baskervilles*. This idiosyncrasy notwithstanding, in *The Adventure of Black Peter* he lectures his long-suffering companion: "There can be no question, my dear Watson, of the value of exercise before breakfast." Yet he further ruins his digestion by staying up all night and consuming "two pots of coffee and an incredible amount of tobacco."

In *The Adventure of the Noble Bachelor* Holmes steps out of character to order what Watson calls "an epicurean little cold supper" (and Holmes eats a lot of cold meals late at night). The menu was a brace of cold woodcock, a pheasant, a pâté de foie gras with a "group of ancient and cobwebby bottles." No mention is made of what these intriguing bottles were — merely that they were old and had obviously been in his cellar for some time.

In *The Adventure of the Veiled Lodger*, Holmes offers Watson another cold meal: "There is a cold partridge on the sideboard and a bottle of Montrachet." Montrachet is, of course, a white wine (an expensive white Burgundy) and while it will go nicely with cold partridge it ought to be chilled and not left standing on the sideboard. In *The Adventure of the Cardboard Box*, on a blazing hot day in August when Baker Street is like an oven,

Holmes and Watson lunch in a restaurant and drink claret. Claret for lunch on a boiling hot day is a sacrilege to those who care about wine.

> *Claret for lunch on a boiling hot day is a sacrilege ...*

Again, in *The Adventure of the Creeping Man*, Holmes remembers an inn called The Chequers where "the port used to be above mediocrity...." Later, Watson writes, "we were, I may say, seated in the old sitting room of the ancient hotel, with a bottle of the famous vintage of which Holmes had spoken on the table between us." Conan Doyle omits to mention the vintage in question, but I would suspect that it was from the 1880s before phylloxera destroyed the vineyards of the Douro Valley.

Englishmen, according to Conan Doyle, drink port and claret while the enemies of Albion drink more exotic stuff, like the Hungarian Imperial Tokay. In *His Last Bow*, the Irish-American spy, Altamont, is described as "having a nice taste in wines," as if to suggest that to discriminate in your taste for wines is somehow unEnglish. But Holmes and Watson are not above polishing off the bottle of Tokay from Franz Josef's own cellar.

More in keeping with Holmes's lifestyle is the meal without wine taken on the run in *The Adventure of the Beryl Coronet*. "He cut a slice of beef from the joint upon the sideboard, sandwiched it between two rounds of bread and thrusting this rude meal into his pocket, he started off upon his expedition."

When Holmes retired to Sussex at the end of his life Watson observed that he devoured sandwiches at irregular hours. The English love bread and sometimes Holmes eats it by itself as he does in *The Five Orange Pips*. Arriving home pale and worn out at 10 o'clock at night, he makes for the sideboard, tears bread from the loaf and devours it with water.

Sherlock Holmes could hardly be called a gourmet. He really cares more about tobacco, coffee, whisky and drugs than he does for the pleasures of the table. In *The Adventure of the Mazarin Stone* Mrs. Hudson asks him when he will be pleased to dine. Holmes replies: "Seven-thirty, the day after tomorrow." But then he was working on a case and that took precedence over other bodily requirements. He can go three days without taking nourishment and he explains why to Watson: "Because the faculties become refined when you starve them. Why surely, as a doctor, my dear Watson, you must admit that what your digestion gains in the way of blood supply is so much loss to the brain. I am a brain, Watson. The rest of me is a mere appendix. Therefore it is the brain I must consider."

... it is the brain I must consider.

In fact, Holmes uses tobacco to inhibit his need for food. In *The Adventure of the Golden Pince Nez* he confesses as to why he smokes: "Ah," he says, "but it kills the appetite."

In *The Adventure of the Dying Detective* he breaks his self-imposed three-day fast with a glass of claret and some biscuits. Alcohol on a stomach that has been empty for three days would have quite an effect! With nothing to stop it, it would hit the blood stream and rocket to the brain. Holmes would have been as high as if he were on cocaine.

Towards the end of his life the detective gives up the little interest he has in food. When Watson visits him in his cottage near Eastbourne the usually amiable doctor grumbles to himself, "The dinner itself was neither well served nor well cooked and the gloomy presence of the taciturn servant did not help to enliven us."

There are other references to alcoholic beverages scattered

through the stories. Curiously the sole mention of champagne is on American soil: in *The Valley of Fear* when the Bodymaster drinks the quarrelling toast of the Lodge with Ted Baldwin, McGinty and McMurdo. In "a garish Italian restaurant" called Goldini's, Holmes and Watson drink coffee and Curaçao with their cigars. Interestingly enough, Conan Doyle does not name his favourite restaurant which appears twice in the stories. It's referred to merely as being in the Strand, so it must have been Simpson's where you can still get the best roast beef in London.

I have dealt at some length with Sherlock Holmes's bizarre dining habits and now I'd like to focus on how his creator used wine and spirits as plot devices. In *A Case of Identity* there is a reference to Mr. Winndibank as being "a traveller in wines for Westhouse and Marchbank, the great claret importers of Fenchurch Street," but his occupation has nothing to do with the story line.

There are only two cases which are solved by Holmes's knowledge of beverage alcohol. In *Black Peter* Holmes is told that there is a tantalus containing brandy and whisky on the sea chest. Yet there are two dirty glasses and a bottle of rum on the table. From this information Holmes makes the following deduction about the killer: "You remember that I asked you whether whisky and brandy were in the cabin. You said they were. How many landsmen are there who would drink rum when they could get these other spirits? Yes, I was certain it was a seaman."

A technical rather than a social knowledge of beverage alcohol was required to crack the case at the Abbey Grange. Here the clue was the beeswing in empty wine glasses. Beeswing is a translucent crust thrown by some vintage ports.

Lady Brackenstall tells Holmes that she had been tied up by three burglars who had killed her husband. They had opened a bottle of wine "to steady their nerves." Holmes examines the empty glasses. "The three glasses were grouped together, all of them tinged with wine, and one of them containing some dregs of beeswing. The bottle stood near them, two thirds full and beside it lay a long, deeply stained cork. Its appearance and the dust upon the bottle showed that it was no common vintage which the murderers had enjoyed."

Holmes declares that "only two glasses were used and that the dregs of both were poured into the third glass, so as to give the false impression that three people had been there. In that way all the beeswing would be in the last glass would it not?"

An ingenious plot point. Except that table wine does not have beeswing and if it were port Conan Doyle would have made the distinction. Only bottle-aged port would throw such a deposit. Port bottles have exceptionally long corks and only a vintage port that had been laid down for many years would have stained the cork that deeply.

In conclusion, Sherlock Holmes and Dr. Watson are men very much of their time and they shared the tastes and prejudices of their class in matters of wine and food. The red wine of Bordeaux, the white wine of Burgundy and port were their beverages at table; whisky and soda and the occasional liqueur with coffee and cigars when they relaxed. Their food was plain — they like roast game birds, chops and roast beef. Their favourite meal was breakfast, which was invariably large. It would appear that the world's greatest detective became addicted to coffee as well as cocaine and while he knew what was good from the vineyards of Europe he did not go out of his way to obtain it.

Wine as Medicine

"Drink no longer water," counsels Paul in his first epistle to Timothy, "but use a little wine for thy stomach's sake and thine often infirmities." The wisdom of the New Testament as expounded by the patron saint of preachers and tentmakers.

> "My doctor advises me to drink two glasses of wine a day. What I consume at night is my business."
> OSCAR WILDE

St. Benedict, who was a stickler for celibacy, advised his brother monks to drink some wine on feast days so that their meals "would always remain digestible and cheerful."

Innocent VIII, the most worldly of twelfth century popes, once wrote to the Duke of Burgundy thanking him for a gift of Beaune wine. The Holy Father confessed that it was "particularly favourable to my temperament. I used it regularly during my last illness."

Although the Koran proscribes the drinking of alcohol for the faithful, it does permit its use for medical purposes. Witness this quote from *The Arabian Nights*, a collection of Oriental folk tales compiled in the mid-fifteenth century: "Wine digests food and disperses care. It dispels flatulence and clarifies the blood. It clears the complexion and quickens the body, heartens the chicken-hearted and fortifies sexual power in men. But to name all its virtues is tedious. In short, had not Allah forbidden it, there is nothing on the face of the earth to stand in its stead."

I could go on with third-party endorsements from the scriptures of the world's great religions as to the salutary effects of wine but I will merely bludgeon the point home with a legend and a historical fact. There are 450 references to wine in the Bible, beginning with Noah's emergence from the ark. The first thing the patriarch did when he set foot on dry land was to plant a vineyard (no kidding! A fellow could do with a drink locked up in a floating zoo all that time). I wonder what variety would suit the terroir on Mt. Ararat?

The founder of the Persian empire, Cyrus the Great, who released the Jews from captivity in Babylon in 539 BC, ten years before his death, would order his troops to purify their drinking water with wine. So too did the Roman legions. It could be argued that the Roman empire lasted as long as it did because of wine. When Caesar's legions conquered the lands north of the Alps they kept healthy by using a ration of one litre a day. They added wine to their water to kill bacteria and applied wine to their wounds to disinfect them. The legionnaires remained fighting fit while the tribes of Gaul and Britannia were wasted with malaria, cholera, typhoid and yellow fever.

... you cannot get typhoid or TB from any wine.

André Simon summed up the virtues of wine very concisely in a monograph written in 1946: "Wine is the safest, pleasantest and most wholesome of beverages. It is safer than water or milk: you cannot get typhoid or TB from any wine, be it old or young, cheap and nasty or rare and costly. No microbes live in wine. It is pleasanter than other safe drinks because it is more gentle as well as varied."

In fact, if wine had been invented in this century (after Prohibition) it would be hailed as a wonder drug.

A wine can be up to 90 per cent water but water and wine are antithetical: otherwise, why the Miracle at Cana when Christ turned water into wine at the wedding feast? Six water pots of stone, according to St. John, containing two or three firkins each.

Now I happen to be planning my own wedding as I write this, so I was curious as to how much wine was needed for the Cana bash. I did some research on how much a firkin contained. The term "firkin," as used in the English translation of the Bible, dates back to the fifteenth century, derived from the Middle Dutch word *vierde*, meaning "fourth." It described a barrel size used by English brewers which had a capacity of 9 imperial gallons, one quarter of a standard normal barrel. Assuming that the six stone pots in question held at least two firkins, then Christ would have turned 108 imperial gallons of water into wine.

It must have been one hell of a party.

There is no antonym for a miracle, in the sense of something you don't want to witness: for instance, the turning of wine into water, although some winemakers of my acquaintance can do this with ease and once in Hong Kong I saw someone put ice cubes into a glass of Château Lafite.

In this matter I agree with the English poet and novelist G. K. Chesterton whose poem on Noah has the following refrain: "I don't care where the water goes if it doesn't get into the wine." (The late Baron Philippe de Rothschild is said to have consumed, every evening, a glass of Château d'Yquem with an ice cube. He considered that the effect of the melting ice enhanced the wine's bouquet. I have never tried this myself — and nor would I with Yquem — but there is a precedent for the practice. Single malt distillers add a little water to their whisky to bring out the bouquet.)

If I am to be damned by some readers for invoking scripture to support my contention that wine is a healthy and health-promoting beverage I will quote now from medical and historical sources. "There is absolutely no scientific proof of a trustworthy kind," wrote George Saintsbury in *Notes On A Cellarbook*, "that moderate consumption of sound alcoholic liquor does a healthy body any harm at all; while on the other hand there is the unbroken testimony of all history that alcoholic liquors have been used by the strongest, wisest, handsomest and in every way best races of all time…." The key word here is *sound*. If the alcohol in question is the product of a natural fermentation without any chemical additives, dyes or preservatives, it is as good as a food. According to the *Encyclopedia Britannica*, "It has been demonstrated that the natural grape sugars in wine are readily absorbed by the human system and are desirable in the diet, that the alcohol in wine is a quick source of caloric energy, that wine has definite blood-building iron content."

Louis Pasteur, the French chemist, considered wine to be the best and healthiest drink for us, containing as it does Vitamins A, B and C and all thirteen trace minerals necessary to support human life; and, what's more, it carries these vitamins in a balance which will not upset the body's metabolism.

… it can stimulate the appetite and can help in dieting.

The various acids in wine make it an ideal antiseptic for use inside the body and a disinfectant outside. Wine acts as a mild and safe sedative; it can kill bacteria in drinking water and on raw meat; it can stimulate the appetite and can help in dieting. On this subject Professor Georges Portmann, a leading European authority on wine and health, has written, "Wine can be used to replace 500 calories of fat or sugar intake in the daily diet. These calories will be completely consumed and will not add an ounce

of weight. Some employed wine is very useful in reducing — it
being understood that the food intake will be reduced by the 500
calories replaced by the wine." And don't be misled by the old
wives' tale that red wine is more fattening than white. The calorie
content of wine is related to its alcohol and residual sugar content. The higher the alcohol, the higher the calorie count. A
Beaujolais with 11 per cent alcohol will have less calories than a
California Chardonnay at 12.5 per cent alcohol.

Wine also helps you to digest a meal since the acid in wine is
similar in its pH to our stomach acid. If you want to stimulate
appetite, a dry white wine, dry sherry or Brut champagne is ideal
since the acidity will activate the glands and make your mouth
literally water. On the other hand, a sweet wine taken before a
meal will dull the appetite since the sugar will go some way to
satisfying your need for food.

Alexis Lichine's *New Encyclopedia of Wines & Spirits*, the bible
of the trade, has a chapter on Wine and Health: "Considered as
food alone, a bottle of natural wine a day is the desirable average
for a person of normal size, although for one not engaged in man-
ual labour a little less wine (say half a litre) may be sufficient.
While providing about one sixth of required nourishment it cannot add weight."

Let's consider what wine can do for the heart. We are all famil-
iar with The French Paradox (a nation that consumes so much
animal fat — foie gras, cheeses, butter, cream — has the lowest
incidence of heart disease in the industrialized world, thanks to
its consumption of red wine). Even the Canadian and United
States governments have reluctantly come to the realization that
two glasses of red wine a day can be beneficial in terms of pro-
moting health.

The human body can absorb, metabolize and turn into energy
one gram of alcohol for every kilogram of body weight, provided
that the alcohol is taken with food over the period of the day. In
general terms, a healthy body can metabolize a glass of wine in 75

minutes. Food in the stomach delays alcohol absorption into the blood stream and gives the liver time to oxidize it. Residual sugar in sweet wines also delays absorption while carbonic gas in sparkling wines speeds up the process — which means that Château d'Yquem takes longer to produce any effects of inebriation than Krug.

Just how much wine is a sensible amount to take? Most doctors today, being conservative in these matters, will recommend no more than 8 ounces a day, or in other words, two or three small glasses. In so doing they are following an ancient precedent, whether they know it or not. A Greek master chef, Athenaeus, a native of Nauticus in Egypt who lived in Rome around AD 200, wrote a mammoth work on gastronomy called *Deipnosophistae*, "The Banquet of the Learned." On this subject he wrote:

> The cups of wine a prudent man may take:
> The first of them for constitution sake,
> The second, to the girl he loves the best,
> The third and last, to lull him to rest.
> Then home to bed. But, if a fourth he pours,
> That is the cup of folly, and not ours.
> Loud noisy talking on the fifth attends,
> The sixth breeds feuds and falling out of friends;
> Seven begets blows and faces stained with gore.
> Eight, and the watch patrol breaks ope the door;
> Mad with the ninth, another cup goes round,
> And the swilled sot drops senseless to the ground.

But perhaps the seventeenth century English poet, William Lithgow, said it best. And so well his words should be engraved over every wine store on the continent.

> He that eateth well, drinketh well.
> He that drinketh well, sleepeth well, sinneth not;
> He that sinneth not goeth straight through Purgatory to Paradise.

If I have not convinced you, as I have myself, that Wine Is The Best Medicine, then you should read Frank Jones's *The Save Your Heart Wine Book,* which explains in great detail how wine protects you from heart disease. It all has to do with a natural component of grapes called "resveratrol." This natural anitifungicide found in the skins of grapes has been known to the Chinese as a folk remedy called *kojo-kon.* Resveratrol, researchers have discovered, is an antioxidant that increases High Density Lipoprotein cholesterol in the blood stream and eliminates the harmful Low Density Lipoprotein cholesterol which causes build-up of fat in the arteries. Hence the idea that a couple of glasses of red wine will stop your heart from attacking you.

On a more jocular note you might pick up a copy in a second hand book store of Dr. Emmerick A. Maury's book that he wrote in 1974, entitled *Wine Is The Best Medicine.* The French doctor suggested what specific wines might be used as "supplementary medicines" for individual complaints and conditions. In his preface he summed up his theme in this mellifluous phrase: "the natural therapeutic effects of a well-chosen wine." Being French, he naturally selected all French wines. He explained the chemical composition of each and its medical properties which might help to alleviate certain conditions. I have chosen a few to reproduce here.

Rheumatism — Recommended wines — Dry light wines such as the natural (non-carbonated) wines of Champagne. Why? Because they are rich in sulphur and mineral elements. Dosage: two glasses per meal.

Tonsillitis — Recommended wines — Red Bordeaux wines from the Médoc region. Why? Because the tannin content of these wines gives them decongestant qualities and also because, like all wines, they are bactericidal, antiseptic, tonic and diaphoretic. Dosage: warm up 500 grams of 10 per cent wine chosen according to the taste of the patient. Add 10 grams of cinnamon, sugar and lemon peel: drink two half bowlfuls three times a day.

Pregnancy — Recommended wine — light red, 10 per cent Bordeaux wines. Why? Because the light red Bordeaux is rich in calcium and oenotannins, and also because it facilitates anti-toxic liver functions. Dosage: two glasses per meal.

Fever — Dr. Maury prescribes a bottle of Dry or Brut champagne, a glass every hour. At the risk of bringing on your symptoms I will run quickly through his cures for other common conditions.

Diarrhoea — Beaujolais, four glasses a day.

Gout — Sancerre, four glasses a day (or Pouilly-Fumé, Provence Rosé)

Menopause — St. Émilion, four glasses a day

Anaemia — Graves, four glasses a day

The question springs to mind, what happens if the patient enjoys the treatment and over-medicates himself? The unrepentant Dr. Maury, in true Gallic fashion, has an answer to this. He quotes a colleague: "If the danger of alcoholism exists in France as everywhere else...it is due not to the consumption of wine but rather its too infrequent usage."

In Praise of Older Wines

> "To air is human; to decant, divine."
> ALEXANDER POPE

Question: To what or to whom do the following quotations refer?

"Raspberry scented like the breezes from the Islands of the Blessed, a dream of grace and delicacy, the twinkling feet of dancing nymphs suddenly set free in our tedious world…"

"They opened the gates of Paradise which Swinburne fathered on Swedenborg where all the senses were confounded and where music, colour and perfume were one."

Believe it or not, both refer to bottles of wine. Not just any old wine. These panegyrics were penned, without the hint of a blush, by two British connoisseurs in the 1940s. They refer to a tasting of Château Margaux 1871 and Château La Lagune 1858 respectively, wines made during the golden age of claret before the dreaded phylloxera destroyed the vines of Europe. They say that Bordeaux wines have never been quite as good since. (But then, they always say that about golden ages.)

If you have ever had to pour a wine down the sink because it tasted like bilge water you're probably asking yourself how a wine can live for a hundred years or more and still be drinkable, let alone elicit such dotty prose. Well, certain wines from years when the climate was perfect — a mixture of rain and sunshine in sufficient quantities during the growing season, a long hot summer and low yields, perfectly ripe grapes that contain the right balance of sugar, acidity and tannin — can keep on going like an ageing trouper.

I doubt if we will ever see 100-year-old claret after the 1975 vintage. That was the year when virtually every château went over to destemming their grapes to cut down the amount of tannin in the wine. Tannin is what gives red wine its ability to age for many years. We don't have the patience today to wait a generation for our wines to come around. Most of us would like to drink them in our own lifetime.

But even with modern vinting techniques there are certain wines that will last long enough to hold for a newborn's twenty-first birthday. Reliable candidates are the top growths of Bordeaux in a good year, certain Burgundies, the sweet wines of Germany, the finest Barolos, Barbarescos, Rioja reds and some Rioja whites, top Vouvrays and other Chenin Blanc–based wines from the Loire, Château-Chalon, Riesling Icewine, Tokaji, to say nothing of such fortified wines as port, sherry and madeira. There are, of course, anomalies. I recall Patrice Noyelle of Mommessin serving me in the company's cellar in Mâcon a bottle of 1947 Moulin-à-Vent in 1987. Beaujolais has no right to last that long, but in a fantastic year like '47 it did — and it tasted like a mature Beaune!

There is a curious thing that happens to old red wines. The

We don't have the patience today to wait a generation ...

intrinsic character of the grape blurs and when they are tasted blind it is very difficult to tell the difference between an old claret (Cabernet Sauvignon) and an old Burgundy (Pinot Noir), or for that matter a Hermitage (Syrah) from the Rhône, a venerable Barolo (Nebbiolo) or an aged Rioja (Tempranillo). The colour fades to brick with an orange hue at the rim. They take on organic smells of leather, truffle, coffee bean and chocolate and the sweetness of the fruit sings through. But the characteristic flavour of the variety is no longer discernible.

There is a curious thing that happens to old red wines.

In 1982 the British Columbia–based wine importing company, Mark Anthony Wines, held a tasting of Château Margaux 1888 and 1892 at the Sutton Place hotel in Toronto. Both wines were very much alive with intense bouquets of sweet tobacco. The younger of the two still had good fruit, lively acidity and a touch of tannin.

When I was living in London I used to spoil myself on my birthday (we Taureans do that kind of thing) by purchasing a special bottle from Andrew Lowe Fine Wines, a company that specializes in rare bottles. Usually, I chose a 1945 which was perhaps the best year this century for just about everything everywhere (1990 is the next great year virtually everywhere). The Chambertin and Cheval Blanc stand out in my memory. Interestingly enough, Lowe had on his list in the 1970s a 1935 Bohemian Club Cabernet Sauvignon, a 1937 Larkemeade Zinfandel and a 1939 Louis

The Chambertin and Cheval Blanc stand out in my memory.

Martini Cabernet Sauvignon, all from California.

Why, you may be asking yourself, is he tantalizing me with wines I may never be able to taste? Sheer perversity on my part. I've been reading accounts of the 1900 Bordeaux vintage (as we approach the millennium) — picking date September 24, very abundant, very good quality. "One of the most perfect vintages ever," according to Michael Broadbent. Five stars. (Perhaps 2000 will be another such vintage.) This is not oenological masochism. I look at it this way: I have never heard Paganini play the violin or seen Sarah Bernhardt act on stage, but reading about their performances gives me vicarious pleasure. An Irish essayist, Robert Lind, once wrote a piece entitled, "On Never Going to the British Museum" in which he makes the point that there are some wonderful things in this world and one derives pleasure from knowing they are there, even if one never gets the opportunity to experience them — and all the more when they are just around the corner.

This is not oenological masochism.

Wine enthusiasts cannot help being curious about the golden age of claret — wines made in Bordeaux between 1860 and 1880 before the dreaded vine disease phylloxera (Greek for "dry leaves") laid waste the vineyards of Europe.

My researches into these wines have, for the most part, been second-hand (or should I say second-throat?).

... I am moved to a frenzy of carpet-biting envy.

When I come across descriptions of them in old wine books I am moved to a frenzy of carpet-biting envy. Here's one written in 1948 by Colonel Ian Maxwell Campbell in a book called *Wayward Tendrils of the Vine*: "Although I prefer 1875 as a vintage for all round excellence, it did not in my opinion produce any one wine to equal the 1864 Lafite, the finest claret I ever tasted." The book jacket describes Colonel Campbell as "a lifelong connoisseur of wine; he firmly believes that wine is a gift of Providence ordained to promote health of mind and body, and worthy of artistic enjoyment."

But back to phylloxera, the disease of the vine that is currently marching through Napa and Sonoma. It has been determined that the phylloxera louse was imported into Europe on North American rootstock, most likely on a variety called Isabella which is resistant to downy mildew. The tiny yellow phylloxera aphid feeds on the sap in the roots of vines and secretes a saliva that prevents the wound from healing. Eventually the vine dies.

Phylloxera's depredations were first discovered in the Southern Rhône regions of Gard and Vaucluse. From there the disease spread like a conquering army throughout the vineyards of Europe. In his history of wine in nineteenth century France and Italy, *The Red & The White*, Leo Loubère has written the best account of the blight's devastating effects:

> Ignoring all hierarchy, [phylloxera] destroyed the finest and the meanest vines, the noble and the proletarian. There were no truly safe areas in France or Italy where vines could take refuge, save in a few sandy places; moreover the invasion hit both countries at almost the same time and with equal destructiveness. The blight did spread slowly in the peninsula, not because the Italians put up better defences, but because…they were briefly safeguarded by their past, by the viticulture their Roman ancestors had left them centuries ago.

France recovered from the Franco-Prussian War (1870-1871) in six years, states Loubère, but it took over a generation to restore their vineyards. The total cost of the phylloxera disaster to France was two and a half times that of the war! Ironically, it was the agent of the blight that turned out to be the saviour of Europe's wine industry. The native North American rootstock that transported the phylloxera louse to Europe was immune to its destructive power. Today, virtually all the wines of Europe are grown on North American rootstock.

If you're looking for a special bottle to celebrate your hundredth birthday, probably the best place to look for it is not in Bordeaux, the Loire, Germany, Madeira or Jerez but in the Crimea.

In April 1990 Sotheby's in London auctioned a selection of wines from the private cellar and winery of Tsar Nicholas II, known as the Massandra Collection. Virtually all of them were sweet. These wines included Massandra Malaga 1914 and Prince Golitzin Lachrima Christi 1896, an 1880 "Seventh Heaven" and an 1886 "Honey of Altae Pastures," one of the wines served at Nicholas II's coronation, as well as twenty-four bottles of the historic 1917 vintage, harvested just in time before the peasants left the vineyards to revolt.

...a special bottle to celebrate your hundredth birthday...

Some 13,000 bottles were disposed of that day for close to £1.5 million; but this number was a mere drop in the bucket compared to the wines still in Massandra's three-tiered, mountainside cellars in the Crimea. The story of these wines is worthy of a novel.

The story of these wines is worthy of a novel.

Nobody knows exactly when the Massandra collection was established, but the impetus came from a Sorbonne-trained lawyer and multi-linguist, Prince Lev Sergeivich

Golitzin. In the 1870s Golitzin set up an estate called Novy Set close to Sudak in the Crimea, not far from the Tsar's summer palace at Livadia; and over the next two decades he devoted himself to making wines and "champagne." So good was his sparkling wine that he was awarded the Grand Prix in Paris in 1900, beating out many of the established French champagne houses!

In spite of this accolade, Golitzin decided that the future of the Crimea lay in dessert and fortified wines and he looked to Spain, Portugal, Hungary and Italy for his inspiration. The Crimea already grew such varieties as Sémillon, Aligoté, Pedro Ximenez and Cabernet Sauvignon, thanks to Count Mikail Voronstov who planted them in the 1820s to service his winery at his Alupka Palace.

When Tsar Nicholas II set up a winery near his summer palace at Massandra in the early 1890s, Prince Golitzin was appointed winemaker and he presided over the cellars until his death in 1915. In 1898 Golitzin hired a winemaker named Alexander Yegorov. Yegorov had survived the Revolution and lived to the age of ninety-five thanks to the patronage of Anastas Ivanovich Mikoyan who, in 1936, invited him to consolidate several of the state-owned wineries under Massandra's control.

But back to the collection that now numbers over a million bottles. During his lifetime, Prince Golitzin bought a lot of wine in Europe and he donated much of it to the Tsar's cellar at Massandra along with the wines he had made himself. The oldest bottle in the cellar is a Spanish sherry dated 1775. His purpose in establishing the cellar was to create a permanent resource for studying the ageing effects of fine wines — the better to improve quality — as well as to amass com-

> *The oldest bottle in the cellar is a Spanish sherry dated 1775.*

mercial quantities of mature wines ready for sale. Approximately 10,000 bottles are added to the collection each year, the only stipulation being that they must be at least ten years old.

You might have thought that the collection would have found its way down Bolshevik throats after the Revolution, but miraculously it survived, thanks to the simple expedient of bricking up the tunnels in which the wines were stored. When the Red Army took control of the Crimea in November 1920 the collection was discovered intact. (A similar ruse was employed by the Paris-based wine company Nicholas, who foiled the occupying Nazis during the Second World War by concealing the entrance to the second level of their cellars where they kept their oldest and rarest wines.)

In 1922 Stalin ordered all the wines found in any of the Tsar's palaces, including those in Moscow, St. Petersburg and Livadia, to be brought to Massandra. Though there was a hiatus in the early and middle 1920s during which no wines were added to the collection (when the Soviets took control there was no one who knew how to make fine wine), the vintages of the late 1920s are said to be "exceptional." Apart from 1930 — a dog of a year everywhere — there is an unbroken continuity of vintages from 1928 to 1940.

... the entire vintage ... was dumped into the Black Sea ...

With the threat of a German invasion of Crimea in 1941, Mikoyan instructed Alexander Yegorov to evacuate the entire collection. Anyone who has had to move a cellar of several hundred bottles knows what agonies this can mean. The final shipment left Yalta on September 21 for Tbilisi in Georgia. German troops entered Yalta on November 8. Because the 1941 wines were still in the vats and could not be transported, the entire vintage, along with other bulk wine reserves, was dumped into the Black Sea, "turning it red as far as the eye could see," wrote one observer.

In October 1944 Yegorov began the Herculean task of shipping the wines back to the Massandra cellars from three separate locations. When Stalin, Churchill and Roosevelt met in the White Hall of the Livadia Palace at Yalta in February 1945, all the bottles were back in place. (As a vinous footnote to history, the three leaders all stayed in Tsarist palaces: Stalin at Massandra, Churchill at Alupka, and Roosevelt at Livadia, each with its own place in Russian wine lore.)

Today, Massandra produces twenty-four different styles of wine, mainly in the sweet and dessert categories, many of which can live for 100 years or more. The Crimea's south coast where the vineyards are located — a 70-kilometer strip between the mountains and the Black Sea — is in a sub-tropical zone where the Muscat grape has been raised for 2,500 years. No wine is produced at Massandra now, but the historic facility acts as a bulk and bottle ageing centre for most of the south coast wineries' production. The consortium also includes four large grape-growing estates and two other wineries.

Massandra controls some 12,000 acres of vines producing grapes mostly for sweet or fortified wines. Massandra Red Port, for instance, is made from the Rhône variety Mourvèdre and the local Saperavi (meaning "drier"); Livadia Red and White Port, from Cabernet Sauvignon; while other sweet white ports are fermented from the white Kokour grape or a combination of Sémillon, Aligoté, Pedro Krymsky and the Tokaji varieties, Furmint and Hárslevelü.

White, Black and Rosé Muscats are perhaps the jewels of the Massandra collection, first produced in fortified style at Livadia in 1891 from late harvest grapes. Three styles of "madeira" are made, one in a drier style from Sercial and Verdelho grapes with the local Albillo Krymsky, containing 30 grams per litre residual sugar, and two sweeter styles and some Tokajis from the Hungarian varieties mentioned above.

In 1995 I acquired a bottle of the 1939 Massandra White Muscat. The colour was amber with olive tints. The nose had a white chocolate sweetness which followed through on the palate; the driving acidity cleansed the palate of its honeyed sweetness and prolonged the taste in the mouth for a long time.

China

THE ANCIENT CITY OF GUILIN, WHOSE BLUE MOUNTAINS RESEMBLE JADE hairpins, offers a remarkable cuisine. According to my guide book, "Local restaurants serve snake soup, turtle, masket civet, bamboo rat and pangolin (a scaly ant-eater), which can be washed down with snake bile wine."

I never made it to Guilin during my trip to China in August 1988 but had I done so I doubt if I would have had the courage to eat. As it was, the trip had been marked by a great deal of eating — I had just come from Hong Kong's Food Festival where an international group of wine writers had been invited to "marry" Western wines with Peking, Sichuan, Shanghai, Cantonese and Chiu Chow cuisine (for the results of our tastings see page 175.)

Over two days we sampled twenty dishes and had a cellar of thirty French, Italian, German, Californian and Australian wines from which to select two wines to complement each dish.

Why, I wondered, were no Chinese wines offered? Was it a comment on the state of the Chinese wine industry or on our perception of it?

In the whole vast country there were at the time only some 300,000 acres of vineyards. But more were being planted every year. In a magazine article I wrote that year, headed "The East Is Not Red...Not Yet, But The Future Looks Rosé," I predicted that within ten years wine drinkers around the world would be looking to China as a source of new, inexpensive wines. Well, this has not yet come to pass. My crystal ball needs retooling, but I am convinced it will happen. The People's Republic has the climate, the land and the manpower to produce wine inexpensively, once the initial investment has been made. All it needs is the technology, the expertise, the right grapes planted in the right soils and mesoclimates — and time. Western corporations were already in China when I was there, backing this judgement with their investment dollars.

... wine drinkers around the world would be looking to China ...

The country's three top wineries all had Western partners. Yan Tai and Tsingtao wineries, each producing 30 million bottles a year, were involved with Japanese and English interests respectively. Dynasty, perhaps the best known Chinese wine, grown outside Beijing, is a joint venture with the Rémy-Martin group producing some 120,000 cases of red and white, one-third of which is exported.

The first time I tasted Chinese wine was at a banquet in 1978 in one of Toronto's long-established Chinese restaurants, Sai Woo. The screwtop bottles, bedecked with turquoise and gold labels and red ribbons, were simply called Chinese Red Wine and Chinese White Wine. No indication of the grape type or where they were grown. Both were sweet and highly alcoholic, not unlike the Ontario ports and sherries of a decade earlier.

My next taste of Chinese wines was ten years later, on the three-hour flight from Hong Kong to Beijing. I was served Chefoo White, made by the Chang Yu Pioneer Wine Company. (This wine has a long tradition behind it: Chang Yu established the first

Chinese winery in 1896 at Yantai in northern Shandong province.) The screwcap bottle was still adorned with red ribbons. The wine was lukewarm, sweetly aromatic with a heavy, grapy, alcoholic taste.

At Beijing's 30-storey Kunlun Hotel on the Liang Ma River I browsed the supermarket on the ground level and found, along with poetically-named wines such as Dragon's Seal and Spring Moon, both Changli Cabernet Sauvignon and Tsingtao Riesling. The references to specific grape types were a big leap forward from the days of "Red" and White" wine. The next day I was driven out to visit the Dynasty operation in Tianjin, 160 kilometres south-east of the capital.

The drive takes you past endless rice paddies and brick factories. The two-lane highway is clogged with vintage Russian army trucks, brick-laden donkey carts and bicycles, bicycles, bicycles. Two hours out of Beijing the traffic finally thins and the scenery changes to peach orchards and fields of sunflowers. Our driver is unfamilar with the area and frequently asks directions. Everyone is willing to point the way. After several face-saving, inaccurate directions we finally arrive at the village of Xing Dian Gong Lu.

The white-washed winery, behind its brick wall, looks like an enormous factory. Huge red characters set on the roof of the main building proclaim, "Sino-French Joint Venture Winery." The China National Cereals, Oils & Foodstuffss Import/Export Corporation owns 62 per cent. For its 38 per cent share Rémy Martin invested $1.8 million (US) in working capital, equipment and technical support, including the services of a winemaker. By the second year of operations, the wines under the Dynasty label were already showing a profit, perhaps because Dynasty quickly cornered the *yam sing* market.

Yam sing is the Chinese custom of endless bottoms-up toasts, traditionally drunk with Mao-t'ai, a vicious white spirit distilled from millet and wheat that makes grappa taste like nectar. Mao-t'ai has taken its toll on generations of diplomats and visiting businessmen, all of whom now yearned for something that would allow pledges of friendship and the lining of the throat to co-exist.

The only sight that suggests the real purpose of the plant is a small experimental vineyard outside the office building, planted with Chardonnay, Sauvignon Blanc, Pinot Noir and Merlot.

The winery's general manager, Xu Wen Heng, invites me and my interpreter, Rémy's salesman Albert Tsui Chi Keung, into his spacious office. In one corner is a bed, discreetly hidden by a few strategically placed potted plants. (During the crush winemakers the world over have been known to sleep next to their fermentation vats.) Over cups of green tea he tells me about the operation. The harvest is fixed for September 12. They will buy in 1,500 tons of grapes from local farmers which will make 1 million bottles of medium dry and extra dry white wine (from Muscat de Hambourg, known locally as Dragon's Eye), a dry red and a "Beaujolais" (from Cabernet Sauvignon), and a rosé (Carignan).

"We also make Dynasty Nouveau," Mr. Xu tells me proudly. "Our wine is sold to all China."

Yet Dynasty, for all its success in the market, has a problem — one it shares with every other winery in China. The grapes planted by the Russians in the 1950s for winemaking are also good to eat. The peasant farmers would rather sell them in the marketplace as table fruit (where they would get more money than selling them to the co-operative). Furthermore, the annual grape harvest coincides with the Festival of the Moon when it is traditional for the Chinese to eat grapes.

Not only is it difficult to buy in sufficient qualities of grapes, but what they do get is not always ripe enough. Horacio Reyner Portes, Rémy's Mexican winemaker at that time, complains that the local party leaders often fix an early harvest date so that their workers can move on to other crops. For Portes, a Bordeaux-trained oenologist, this means he has to work with grapes low in sugar and chaptalisation becomes the norm.

In addition, Dynasty's grapes are grown in a region that has a high water table. This means that the roots suck up the moisture, swelling the berries and diluting the sugars, acids and skin pigmentation. As a result, Chinese red table wines grown on flat ground are generally light in colour, without much body and flavour — a deep rosé rather than a full-blooded red.

Mr. Xu orders in the Dynasty whites and rosé for our lunch with several of the winery managers. The German-shaped bottles all carry a label that looks like a still from a Disney cartoon — a stylized mountain landscape with vineyards. The medium dry white has a bouquet of sweet melon. The wine is soft with a distinct flavour of Muscat and a touch of acid on the finish.

The Extra Dry version is clean and full-bodied, more like an Ontario dry Riesling in character. The rosé is orange-salmon in colour with a taste of strawberries, slightly sweet but nicely balanced with acidity. They don't have the structure of a German Riesling or a Tavel rosé, but with the soy sauce, ginger and garlic in the dishes they stand up very well. Better, in fact, than some of the European wines we chose for the Hong Kong banquet.

THE HONG KONG FOOD FESTIVAL BANQUET, 1988

PEKING CUISINE:
   Panfried Bamboo Shoots and Walnuts with Dried Conpoy and
      Chilli Leaves
   Wehlener Sonnenuhr Riesling Spätlese Halbtrocken 1985
   Callaway Vineyard Sauvignon Blanc 1986

   Peking Duck
   Simi Cabernet Sauvignon 1983
   Villa Antinori Chianti Classico Riserva 1983

SICHUAN CUISINE:
   Sauteed Diced Chicken and Scallops with Dried Chilli "Kung-
      Po" Style

Robert Mondavi Napa Valley Chardonnay 1985
Petaluma Chardonnay 1986

Panfried Prawns with Chilli Sauce
Antinori Castello della Sala 1986
Hugel Gewürztraminer 1986

SHANGHAI CUISINE:
Braised Chin-Hwa Ham with Honey Sauce
Assmannshauser Höllenberg Spätburgunder Spätlese
 Trocken 1985
Coldstream Hills New Pinot Noir 1987

CANTONESE CUISINE:
Shark Fin Soup with Crab Meat and Coral
Robert Mondavi Napa Valley Chardonnay 1985
Tavel Rosé 1987

Steamed King of the Sea
Coldstream Hills New Pinot Noir 1987
Petaluma Chardonnay 1986

CHIU CHOW CUISINE:
Poached Sliced Whelk in Clear Soup

Antinori Castello della Sala 1986
Callaway Vineyard Sauvignon Blanc 1986

Braised Sliced Abalone with Assorted Meat
Louis Jadot Beaujolais-Villages 1986
Assmannshauser Höllenberg Spätburgunder Spätlese
 Trocken 1985

Fortified Wines

> **"A good hemlock, but not a great hemlock."**
> SOCRATES

Beverage alcohol, like clothing and pop music, is subject to the cycle of fashion. Just as there is a current vogue for the Martini after a couple of decades of popular neglect, so too do wines become faddish. Port, after some years in the doldrums, is enjoying a new-found interest. Especially with the 1994 vintage, which is the best certainly since 1977 and possibly since 1963.

I have a vested interest in '94 since I had a foot in it. At Quinta do Bom Retiro Pequeno in 1994 I stripped down to my swimming trunks and a T-shirt and got into the lagar to stomp grapes with the local pickers. The feeling of treading the freshly harvested grapes is rather like wading through lukewarm porridge. The stems scratch your legs and the juice stains your skin.

God made the human foot for the express purpose of crushing grapes. The soles of our feet are strong enough to crush the skins and extract the juice and pulp from the berries but elastic enough not to break the pits and stalks which would add excessive tannin to the fermenting must.

I joined the treaders for their final two hours of free-style cavorting in the lagar. They danced around the place, smoking and listening to a football match on portable radios held to their ears. They had already done the disciplined two hours of marching up and down, arms linked across shoulders, the treading tempo called out by the leader on one end of the line who beats time with a short stick against the granite wall of the lagar.

At Calem in Pinhâo, the treaders, all men, wear a uniform of red plaid shirts and blue shorts. At the end of the compulsory two hours they suddenly break out of martial mode and sing a traditional song called *Liberdad*: "Liberty, ah liberty. Only to the few you're known. If only I had liberty just to call my feet my own."

The English and the Portuguese houses have diametrically opposed views as to what constitutes port. For the traditional English houses — Taylor, Dow, Graham, Cockburn, Warre, etc. — the first duty of port is to be vintage and if it can't be vintage (bottled after two years in great years), at least LBV (late bottled vintage, aged four to six years in wood and then bottled with a vintage date). For the Portuguese true port is aged tawny, what they call Colheita. Be that as it may, the chic drink for the Portuguese man-about-town is Scotch on the rocks which is cheaper in Oporto restaurants than a glass of 20-year-old tawny.

With the rise in popularity of port can sherry be far behind?

Sherry is like Cervantes' *Don Quixote*. Everybody knows it but nobody's read it. Everybody says they like sherry but hardly anyone in North America drinks it. There is a good reason for this. The wine industries on this continent used to make "sherry" from Labrusca grapes that was highly alcoholic and sweet enough to warrant a warning label from the Dental Association. In Ontario in the 1970s these confections were known as "Block and Tackle" wines. You drank a bottle, walked a block and you could tackle anybody.

But true sherry, from Jerez de la Frontera and Sanlúcar de Barrameda, is one of the world's great drinks and now that old Madeira prices are rocketing upwards, sherry is currently the least expensive fine wine going. If you haven't tried the single Almacenista sherries of Emilio Lustau, you have missed something special. I know of no other wine company whose products display a consistent level of quality through the complete range. And Lustau can field some thirty sherries, from the delicate, fresh, camomile-flavoured Reserva Puerto Fino to the tooth-rotting sweetness of the Centenary Pedro Ximenez "Murillo." I once tasted the range at the bodega situated within the old Moorish walls of Jerez, while the winemaker played his guitar.

I prefer Lustau's drier styles: the immaculate Almacenista Manzanilla Pasada de Sanlúcar, bone dry with a crisp, roasted hazelnut flavour and unconscionable length, the Almacenista Oloroso de Jerez "Anada 1918" with its rancio and vanilla nose and intense chocolate and coffee bean flavours, and the Single Cask Palo Cortado Vides with its deep bronze colour, vanilla and caramel nose and mouthfilling coffee flavour.

I don't have to be a soothsayer to predict that sherry will soon enjoy its rightful place in the sun.

... sherry will soon enjoy its rightful place in the sun.

Now the Marsala of Sicily, that's another kettle of fish. The only time most people try Marsala is whipped into egg yolks as Zabaglione. I had my first taste of it in Palermo in 1964 when I visited the island with my parents. I enjoyed it so much I bought a small wooden keg of the stuff they sell to tourists.

The reason we were in Sicily in the first place was to visit a family my parents had met three years earlier while vacationing at Abano, a spa in Italy. At the hotel they met a couple from Palermo and although they had no common language among them they quickly became fast friends, using hand signals, smiling a lot, nodding and laughing together. So much so that the Italian couple invited my parents to come to Sicily the following year to celebrate the marriage of their eldest son.

My stepfather, the lawyer, decided that he would teach himself Italian in the meantime so that he could deliver a speech at the wedding. He bought the necessary books and tapes and studied diligently before composing his address for the assembled guests. The thrust of his speech was respect for grandparents (a theme close to his heart and one that would appeal to Sicilians). His words, according to my mother, were greeted with rapturous applause. Everyone, she told me, was on their feet, applauding and voicing their approval, as if he had just sung "Nessun Dorma" like Pavarotti. His speech was even reprinted in the local newspaper.

"Where," they asked him, "had he learned his Italian?"

"From books," said my father.

"Ah," they nodded, "You sounded just like Il Duce."

The books that he had bought were twenty years out of date, using the style and idiom of the language of Benito Mussolini.

Notwithstanding, my parents returned to Sicily two years later and invited me to join them there in June. They would be flying to Rome from Montreal and I would fly from London. We were met at the airport in Palermo by three long black limousines driven by men in heavy blue overcoats, fedoras and five o'clock shadows. Four generations of the family had come to greet us. It occurred to me that my parents had unwittingly befriended members of the mob.

Second Pressings

> *"It is all wee wee in the end."*
> CONFUCIUS

Wine lovers are born with the collector's gene. I know a woman who collects wine stains. At home tastings she uses a white tablecloth and when it gets stained she embroiders the name and vintage of the wine next to it.

Once you're hooked on the grape you get a little crazy; you begin to amass labels, notes, corkscrews, gadgets and other vinous paraphernalia. In my case it's books. My library groans under the weight of some 700 volumes, most which I have never consulted for information. I just love having them around — rather like never going to the British Museum.

I used to haunt second-hand book stores for old wine books and one day, nearly twenty-five years ago, I struck gold.

In a pile of eight books there was a ledger-like volume measuring roughly twelve inches by eight inches. Its stiff buff cover was printed with the name Berry Bros. Inside, written in black ink in a thin, sloping hand were a series of top growth wines mainly from the 1933 vintage. What I held in my hands purported to be the cellar book for the wine cellar in Queen Mary's dolls' house!

I was curious about the book's origins so I phoned up Berry Bros. and asked to speak to one of the directors. I was put through to Anthony Berry who invited me to the shop in St. James's the following morning. He ushered me into his office and when we sat down I handed him the cellar book. He glanced through it and he told me that it was indeed what it said it was: the handwriting he identified as that of his father, Francis, who had been requested by Buckingham Palace to lay down the wine cellar for the Queen's dolls' house at Windsor Castle.

Everything in the Queen's dolls' house is perfectly to scale, Anthony Berry told me, even down to the straw sleeves that cover the inch-long champagne bottles in the cellar. And each of the bottles contains the precise wine that is listed in the cellar book, syringed into the miniature bottles. The cellar book I had purchased in a second-hand book store was the model from which a reproduction in Lilliputian form was made — in exact proportion to its surroundings.

... my gesture was not entirely altruistic.

I could see that Berry was holding the book lovingly. I looked around the oak-panelled office that reeked of history and tradition. I thought of my book collection and I gazed at the old account ledgers that spoke to the history of the British Empire.

"This book really belongs here," I said. "I would like to present it to you."

I must confess that my gesture was not entirely altruistic. I thought that such a munificent gesture on my part might be rewarded with some really splendid bottles.

"That's very generous of you, old boy," said Berry. "I would like to give you something in return."

Visions of 1927 Taylor's port or a brace of Cheval Blanc 1947 danced before my eyes.

Berry stood up and reached for the shelf above my head. He took down a book, reached for his fountain pen and wrote the following inscription on the fly leaf: "For Tony Aspler... In exchange for the Wine Cellar Book. With best wishes from Anthony Berry, 28 July 1972."

He then handed me the book. It was a copy of *Number Three Saint James's Street* — A history of Berry's the Wine Merchants by H. Warner Allen.

In hindsight I wish I had inscribed the cellar book to Anthony Berry.

Next time you drop by Berry Bros. ask if you can see it. I do hope it's still there.

Enhance your wine experience...
With other books by **TONY ASPLER**

VINTAGE CANADA
THE COMPLETE REFERENCE TO CANADIAN WINES
This popular book includes profiles of all Canadian wineries, along with tasting notes of all the wines from each winery. There is also an expanded section on Canadian icewine.
0-07-552604-2 / $21.99, paperback, 290 pgs.

TONY ASPLER'S WINE LOVER'S COMPANION
ALL ABOUT WINES FROM CANADA'S MOST WIDELY READ COLUMNIST AND AUTHOR
A reference to guide you on how to buy, store, serve and match wine to various foods.
0-07-551840-6 / $21.99, paperback, 246 pgs.

TONY ASPLER'S GUIDE TO NEW WORLD WINES
An easy-to-read, four-star rating system, covering over 15,000 of the finest "New World Wines."
0-07-552661-1 / $14.99, paperback, 144 pgs.

A TASTE FOR WINES
AN AUDIO GUIDE TO THE WORLD OF WINE IN THE COMPANY OF CANADA'S BEST-KNOWN WINE WRITER
Tony talks you through where wine comes from, the different types of wine, how to serve them, and how to cook with them.
1-896668-00-3 / $17.99 Two Cassettes: one hour and 45 minutes

ALIGOTÉ TO ZINFANDEL
EXPLORING THE WORLD OF WINE
This book leads the novice through the A-to-Z of selecting, storing, serving and appreciating the wonderful world of wine. A terrific winelover's reference book.
0-07-551675-6 / $9.98, paperback, 115 pgs.

These books are available at bookstores across Canada. If a book is out of stock, ask your local bookstore to order it from McGraw-Hill Ryerson.